Hollybush

Folk Building and
Social Change
in an
Appalachian
Community

Hollybush

Folk Building and
Social Change
in an
Appalachian
Community

by Charles E. Martin

THE UNIVERSITY OF TENNESSEE PRESS / KNOXVILLE

Publication of this book has been aided by a grant from the American Council of Learned Societies from funds provided by the Andrew W. Mellon Foundation.

Frontispiece: Charles E. Martin

Cloth: 1st printing, 1984.
Paper: 1st printing, 1993.

Sections of this book have appeared in slightly different form in *Appalachia and America: Autonomy and Regional Dependence,* Allen Batteau, ed. (Lexington: Univ. Press of Kentucky, 1983), *Appalachian Journal, Natural History,* and *Pioneer America.*

Library of Congress Cataloging in Publication Data

Martin, Charles E., 1945–
    Hollybush: Folk building and social change in an Appalachian community.
    Bibliography: p.
    Includes index.
    1. Hollybush (Ky.)—Buildings. 2. Vernacular architecture—Kentucky—Hollybush. 3. Architecture and society—Kentucky—Hollybush. 4. Hollybush (Ky.)—Social life and customs. 5. Appalachian Region, Southern—Social life and customs. I. Title.
NA735.H64M37   1984   720'.9769'165   83-10201
ISBN 0-87049-408-2 (cloth: alk. paper)
ISBN 0-87049-816-9 (pbk.: alk paper)

for K.R.M. and for my Father

Acknowledgments

Any study that utilizes oral history is dependent on the cooperation of others. I owe a sincere debt of gratitude to all of those who talked to me about Hollybush—in their homes, on the job, in the grocery, at the gas pump, or after I flagged them down on the road. I owe particular thanks to Ada Caudill, Oliver Caudill, Ollie Craft, Austin Slone, Ellis Slone, Mitchell Slone, Vansel and Meredith Slone, and Mary Sparkman, who were willing to go over Hollybush history until I understood it.

My initial interest in material culture and its interpretive possibilities stemmed from listening to Henry Glassie's penetrating lectures on "American Folk Style" at Indiana University in the early 1970s. I also used Professor Glassie's illustrating techniques as models for my own. Once this work began, Tom and Betsy Adler lent continuous encouragement. Each time Tom said, "But this is neat stuff," he would spur me on for a few more weeks. Ron Daley, then director of the Appalachian Learning Laboratory at Alice Lloyd College, had the presence of mind to leave me alone when he sensed I was becoming possessed with this project. The Alice Lloyd College and Hindman Settlement School Photographic Archives both allowed me use of their historic photographs, and the Oral History Project at the college transcribed the tapes. The Carl D. Perkins Vocational School in Hindman plotted the deeds. I owe them all my thanks.

As this study entered the writing stage, Mary Ellen Brown, Richard M. Dorson, and Robert Gunderson all offered helpful suggestions. Warren Roberts gave not only encouragement but on-the-mark assessments all the way through research and writing. He has been of constant assistance.

After the manuscript was written, Larry Danielson, Ormond Loomis, Lynwood Montell, and Patricia Sterling helped to refine it. Lyn Montell, in particular, championed this history for publication early on. Bless him for being able to see that, unwieldy as it was, it had possibilities.

Many friends, in conversations both pointed and casual, gave me insights into processes of cultural change. I would like to thank Jeemes Akers, Wally Campbell, Kenneth W. Clarke, Jim Leary, John Lewis, Charlotte Madden, Blanton Owen, Bill Phillips, Gail Rosser, Gary Stanton, Al Stewart, and Barry Stevens for their valuable perceptions.

The Appalachian Center at the University of Kentucky lent financial support for additional research and rewriting by awarding me a James Still Fellowship during the summer of 1982. Dr. Ramona Lumpkin and Jean Brymer, members of the staff, were cooperative and helpful critics.

I owe a special debt to Irene Slone, who carries her former community's history in her mind and in her heart. Irene's constant help in sorting out Hollybush's past was invaluable to me.

Charles E. Martin
April 4, 1983

Contents

Figures

Hollybush

Folk Building and
Social Change
in an
Appalachian
Community

Introduction

What follows is an account of a society that found itself confronted by change—not a steady change with an accepted and anticipated pattern, but a stinging change, which created a wary understanding among its participants that the future was going to share little with the past. Small by any measure, this society had lost its sense of continuity with its own history. Yet consciously or not, it recorded parts of this most personal of dramas in predictably stable artifacts and unexpectedly stable memories. With an analysis and synthesis of the two, the society's story, spanning eighty tumultuous years, gradually unfolds.

The chronological record of this eastern Kentucky society, the Head of Hollybush (named for its innermost location in Hollybush hollow, Knott County), is relatively brief. It was settled in 1881 and abandoned in 1960; through the intervening years it built up to a population of about 150 people on thirty farm sites over five hundred to six hundred acres. All that remains of the community today are fields overgrown with honeysuckle and berry briars, hillsides newly wooded with tulip poplar, collapsed and collapsing houses and outbuildings, and chimneys standing mutely in the midst of ashes.

The Head covered about one square mile around three short branches of Hollybush Creek (Fig. 1). Two of the three branches directly connect; the third could be reached from the other two by hiking over a steeply inclined 1,800-foot mountain, or by walking the one and one-half miles around it. The utility company that controls the underground gas in this area opened a road into the Head's branches in the 1930s in order to inspect

its wells. Before that, one traveled in on the narrow paths that run along and through Hollybush Creek or over the surrounding mountains from neighboring communities.

The Head was always difficult to enter. It is isolated in an isolated area, bounded by high-reaching hills resembling the rim of a volcano, which slope steeply down to the thin bottoms the runoff water has carved. Since Hollybush Creek is longer than most tributaries in this section of the county (four miles instead of the usual one or two), the extra distance into the Head and its mountain walls served as barriers against early settlement. After settlement did occur, this sense of enclosure continued to separate the Head from settlements along the lower sections of Hollybush and Caney Creek, the main tributary and area of densest habitation in this part of Knott County. Although trade, friendship, and courtship took place among all local peoples, the Head was seen, by residents and nonresidents, as more remote than the surrounding hollows and communities.

If the Head of Hollybush was so isolated and inconvenient, why did people initially settle there, and why did they remain? First, Hollybush offered inexpensive land, as fertile as the first cleared and plowed bottom along Caney Creek in the early 1800s. Also, when the first settler came over the mountain into the Head in the 1880s, technology and class expectations were the same throughout the area. Everyone on Caney and Hollybush saw the reigning cultural system as subsistence agriculture; a farmer could support himself as well in Hollybush as in any other part of these mountains. Throughout the county it rained the same amount

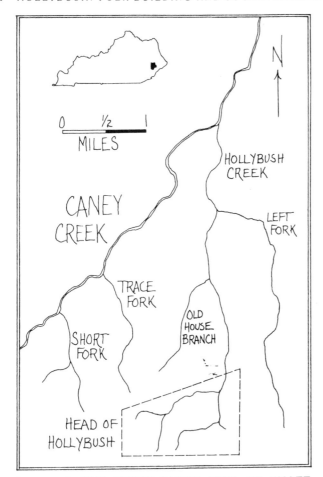

Figure 1. THE UPPER-CANEY AREA OF KNOTT COUNTY, densely mountainous and coal-rich. (All photos and drawings by the author except where noted.)

(about 140 days a year), the hills were as steep, and the soil as rocky.[1] Nearly all people lived in log houses in the level bottoms between the hills, planted corn on the hillsides, and divided their land among the children they abundantly produced.[2] A sense of egalitarianism governed them.

It is common for urban influence and new roads eventually to reach the country farmer, as they ultimately reached Caney Creek, but the physical barriers around the Head could never come down. People remained inside these steep hills by choice, even after becoming aware of the inconvenience and separation. The Head was both birthplace and home for many, and they recognized themselves and each other as sharing and belonging to it. They may have felt apart from their outside neighbors, but their collective concerns—crops, weather, and one another—continued to unite them.

Once settled, why did these close-knit people choose to desert their community? What would have caused a society like Hollybush to die? These were the glaring

questions that remained in 1978 after six months of interviewing former residents and attempting to form some historical description of the social system once in force. If answers could be found to Hollybush's demise, might they suggest patterns of social disruption that could then be applied to other communities? Might we also see, because of Hollybush's diminutive size, the effect of this disruption in personal terms? How, specifically, did these people structure their responses to whatever it was that altered their outlook?

I initially knew I could undertake a study of this area for two reasons. First, theoretical parameters could be more explicit than is usually possible in such studies, since there was a societal end in Hollybush.[3] The pressures that finally caused these people to break with their past must have been traumatic; for the historian, however, clear limits are preferred circumstances. Since history and culture continue dramatically to develop, the threat of new adaptations to new circumstances steadily belies conclusive explanations for each. In the Head of Hollybush, an absolute societal beginning and ending and the forbidding boundaries—a time and place sharply defined—provided clear controls toward historical reconstruction.

Second, the physical remains of log and board structures in Hollybush still gave mute evidence of the community, and could possibly provide clues to the settlement's life and death. Rather than be concerned only with house types and their geographic diffusion, or with compiling comparative cross-regional notes (which create only the illusion of architectural understanding), I found it necessary to make these artifacts speak for history.

How, then, to begin to retell this story? No publications on the community existed except the incomplete descriptions in deeds, census records, and tax lists. The Head was not the type of location to elicit much public curiosity, since the hills so effectively protected it. The farther one goes back, the narrower and darker the road becomes because of frequent slides and looming trees and undergrowth.

Despite the lack of documentation, many former occupants who still hold title to their Hollybush land were living along Caney and could contribute information. Since the area of study and its population were small, it did not take long for their fruitful recollections to overlap and coincide. But these former residents had little knowledge of their community's overall history, nor were they able to offer a sweeping theory as to why what was no longer is.[4] These people, like the rest of us, were locked into the context of their lives and were unable to discern long-range patterns of historical behavior spanning several generations. The rigors and pressures of living take up too much time.

What might carry comprehensive information, though, were the structural artifacts left behind, for as Henry Glassie notes, "Rigorously analyzed, the artifact is always genuine because it is an expression of its maker's mind."[5] Hollybush artifacts, it is true, were in a seemingly sorry state to be used in any analysis; since the Head had been abandoned for twenty years, weather and arson had destroyed most structures, and the remainder were rapidly declining. Despite their condition, a second look showed that many of the surviving log houses had been recently built. A well had the date 1937 chiseled into its stones; one house had its interior walls covered entirely with layers of newspapers dating from the 1940s and '50s; another's chimney stones were bonded with commercial cement, a late substance replacing the clay-and-pebble mortar evident in older surviving dwellings. If houses (and barns) had undergone alterations through time—and folk architecture[6] tends to resist change rather than allow it— these shelters would perhaps suggest the impact of new circumstances upon their builders and could be the key to reconstructing Hollybush's past.

Regardless of architecture's promise, however, a survey[7] and analysis[8] alone could not have recreated the artifactual past of structures long burned, replaced, or decayed. Measuring buildings and sketching floor plans could not have supplied human contextual information: how did personality affect the way a house was built? were people overcome with purpose, or could they maintain a sense of humor about what eventually enveloped them? did they react well to the system in which they lived, or did they test its limits? In Hollybush, as research eventually showed, a house built before 1935 was considerably different from one built after, but a survey could not have dated structures finely enough for a community with so short a history. Finally, a survey could not have explained the structural changes many houses underwent nor the critical reasoning behind these alterations: why, for instance, were more and more windows added? why was interior space increasingly partitioned into smaller units?

Preliminary forays using oral history had already shown that it *alone* would not work either. Much critical information detailing cultural change was not retrievable. Many participants were dead, and as mentioned, those surviving were unable to articulate the totality of what had occurred. In a locale and situation like the Head's, both methodologies—oral history and architectural analysis—were needed; they complement each other once integrated, carefully moving from theory to data to analysis.

The first step in this integration, since most of this study's findings were drawn from architectural information existing only in memory, is to recount how these memories were collected, and then to build a theoretical case for the accuracy of memory in relation to architectural space, arrangement, and materials (Chapter 1). A description of the building techniques chosen by Hollybush residents follows (Chapter 2): what wood types, for example, did they choose for the walls? how did the builders cut, shape, and notch the logs? what were the particular attributes of the notches chosen? how did the builders arrive at the space required for a bedroom or a rear kitchen addition? what did women use for decoration when no commercial decorating materials were available in the area? Aside from the useful ethnographic data obtainable from studying construction techniques, the mechanical patterns described aid in understanding the subtle formative changes that occurred both in housing and society. A knowledge of techniques also assists in understanding the survey of the Hollybush artifacts (Chapter 3) built from settlement to abandonment. Every house (and a representative sample of outbuildings) is listed, including all variations made within the structures: the room additions, delineations, partitions wrought by whims of personality and an altered culture. Also included are the dates of construction; the name of the builder; and the types of wood, notching, flooring, roofing, and heat sources. The survey incorporates the essential information by which Hollybush's history is re-created. Once these architectural data have been lineally arranged (Chapter 4), they begin to clarify the physical displacement that Hollybush underwent while attempting to switch from an agrarian to an industrial, from an extended to a nuclear family, system. We move finally to the analysis of culture (Chapter 5) by synthesizing the pattern of technical change in Hollybush with the emotional. The catalyst to change is identified, and the reaction of the people becomes evident.

Hollybush is unique for such a study in that its traditional architecture does not date from the distant past. In nearly all sections of the United States, folk architecture is so rapidly vanishing from the landscape that locating builders and eyewitnesses to construction, and collecting their verbal accounts of techniques and practices, becomes more nearly impossible each day. Since yesterday was not far from today in Hollybush, there are enough living participants to allow a more assured glimpse into a traditional society's patterns of environmental adaptation and cultural change than a survey of buildings picked for their regional representational qualities could supply. Our memories are often strongly associated with physical space, both natural and manmade: my informants could not articulate the factors that determined change in their lives, but they could recall architectural space with a high degree of accuracy. And although no informants had memory of events that occurred in Hollybush in 1890, for example, they could recall a house built that year which they may have seen for the first time decades later; the memory of the structure was the connecting tissue to that particular time. The man-made object lends form to scattered and seemingly unconnected thoughts. When an object's form is steeped in tradition, it speaks not only for the builder but for all his culture because the traditional object—the traditional building—is the collective culmination of thoughts, problems, and solutions. When the object's form has altered over a period of time, the changes are evidence that the cultural process behind its creation has also been altered. Architectural analysis can discover whether a shift has occurred; verbal history, coming to grips with previously unrealized evidence, can reveal reasons. In the case of Hollybush, the two methodologies provided a nearly total architectural and social reconstruction of a society that immersed itself in tradition and then pushed it aside.

By examining the Head's past, we gauge the shocking impact of new ideas on the folk builder and his community, people whom written history usually overlooks but who are most representative of the commonplace realities from which we all descend. If sweeping change could be charted and explained in a small, cohesive area like Hollybush, then this community's experience might well define past regional patterns. The architectural and social history of this one seemingly insignificant square mile could actually be a delayed microcosm, detailing cultural change and its causes within hundreds of similarly sized communities in Appalachia.

That these isolated people continued to build in log long after other groups had abandoned it was of interest; certain technical information had apparently not vanished, and the collection of such descriptive data would have been justification enough to document the Head of Hollybush. But knowledge of technique does not explain real change. The crucial discovery here is that over a period of years these builders did replace log architecture, couched in comforting tradition, with a new and speedier form of construction. The way informants explain the demands and expectations involved in that decision suggests not a simple case of technical adaptation, but a societal rite of passage, a painful metamorphosis where culture was altered through a violent exchange between the established past and the promising future. This transformation was recorded in the structures with which the Head's inhabitants sheltered themselves as clearly as in a thoughtfully written diary. Each time these people took another step away from the past, it was registered artifactually, reflecting new cultural, economic, and environmental circumstances. In Hollybush, cultural history spanned two divergent eras, and their buildings mirror the users' discomfort with that experience. By diachronically arranging these structures and the memories surrounding them, we can replace abstraction with a more complete understanding of the changing intents of these farmers: scratch a layer of newspaper covering a wall, roll over a shaped log lying near fallen chimney stones, and you sense a temporally distant thought.

Do not mind the detail included here; both its commonplace and its technical parts add up to a compelling human whole. Let us also not judge these Kentucky mountain farmers too harshly for abandoning the agrarian ideal. When they heard the bell toll for them, it was only an echo of what had rung many times before.

1. Reconstructing the Past

Had the Hollybush builder constructed his new home next to his old one instead of over it, had he never torn the old one down, had he drawn on the wall and dated all the modifications he had made, and had all this taken place under a protective dome, then perhaps the observations of contemporary folks could have been cut altogether from this study. Folk builders did not act that way, though. They built in the open air; they replaced old with new; and although they may have quietly delighted in the structural changes they conceived, they rarely wrote down what they had done. More likely they let the altered shelter do their bragging for them. Therefore, since much of the Head's architectural past has vanished (during occupation, original structures were replaced by newer ones, parts of buildings were removed and used elsewhere, and houses were burned down in kitchen fires; after 1960, structures either rapidly weathered and decayed, were burned by arsonists, or were torn apart to reach the milled boards and roof tins usable outside of Hollybush), informants' recollections have been imperative in reestablishing descriptive lines to that past. For example, throughout the winter of 1979 I could not find certain houses a number of people had described, nor could I identify the sites. In the early spring, however, the first vegetation to sprout and bloom included day lilies and apple rose, neither of which grow naturally in this area. The day lilies were planted outside the house and the apple rose usually by the well, informants recalled; therefore, instead of searching for log and stone, I looked for these plants. At all sites the pink and green stood out sharply against the light brown humus, as testament to houses long gone and to the aesthetic expectations of their owners.

As interviewing began, though, it became evident that the memories of my informants would need to be stimulated. Too many years had passed; highlights and abstractions had replaced encompassing description. By assembling slides of existing buildings and their surrounding terrain in the order of the structures as one walks toward a particular hollow, I allowed them the opportunity to visually approximate the journeys they once took a quarter of a century ago and more. One slide of a nondescript section of path evoked this response from an informant intimately acquainted with every foot of the walkway:

I know where it's at. I know where the creek is—I know where the creek bed and everything is at. It shows there, I know where the coal bank is. You see, back in those days electricity hadn't been put into Hollybush. And I had gone to this coal bank to scrape up where people got their winter's coal—this was like in the springtime, you know, after everybody quit burning fires in their chimney, but still yet you used coal, you know, and we would heat these old-fashion coal irons to iron your clothes with. Have you ever talked to anybody about any of that? Well, my mother said that if I would go and take a pail down to the coal bank and get her enough coal to heat up the stove, then she would do the ironing, so I took advantage of that. I'd rather went and pack the coal as to do the ironing. So when I went down to get my coal, I met Bethel coming up the hollow. That's when me and him was dating. And he had been down the creek somewhere, so he helped me get my coal, and he packs it to the house for me. I remember that particular time when we got up to the top of the bank, the coal got heavy, so we sat it down, and we just sat there talking, and we talked and talked, and Mommy comes

Figure 2. IRENE SLONE views her home after a quarter-century.

around to the bank and hollers down at me and says, "If I'm going to do this ironing, you'd better bring the coal on to the house." And well, there's just a lot of little things that it seems like it was yesterday that it happened. It wasn't really—back then you didn't think it was much until after it passes. You find newer ways to do things and then you look back.[1]

Once a particular informant's hollow was reached, photos of neighboring buildings evoked memories of other families, Hollybush history, and personal experiences. Most of each interview, however, was spent viewing recent photos of the informant's house, attempting to match its history to the family's history: for example, when were additions built, who built them, and expressly for what purpose? I also requested that we look over and talk about any family photos containing images of the house or outbuildings in order to determine any changes from the present structure, or details of a building now fallen or missing. Residents in the Head did not take many pictures, though, and never intentionally photographed their houses; when a house appeared, it was as an incidental backdrop to family members—the main focal objects.

The interviewing method that gave the greatest returns, however, was to take informants back into the Head to their old homeplaces. These on-site interviews very much directed themselves, with each new turn in the road bringing more comments and analysis. One house, which I saw only as an inanimate ruin, was perceived somewhat differently by an informant who lived in it in the 1930s and 1940s. To both of us, the house was structurally identical, but as he walked into the now roofless building, he quickly turned toward the southwest corner and said, "There was a bed in that corner. My mother died there in 1944."[2] He did not elaborate, only considering it important that I should know the skeleton of what was surely an intense narrative. Later on in the afternoon, as we drove and walked up the third branch, he offered a flood of local history: personal relationships between inhabitants, customs, farming techniques, and architectural history. The informant described communal "workings" (house-raisings) and hoeings, and told how they abruptly ended in the late 1930s when trucks and buses from the northern factories came into Hindman, the Knott County seat. Loudspeakers, fastened on the vehicle roofs, blared promises of jobs and high wages to those willing to climb aboard. Many did, including several men from the Head. With a change of clothes and a bagged lunch, they were hauled out of the county (many never returning except to visit), shattering a social structure that perhaps had outlived its time.

On another day an informant who had lived in this same house twenty-five years earlier[3] described it quite differently by recalling its earlier form (see Chapter 3,

Nos. 6 and 28; all subsequent identification of artifacts by number will refer to the list in Chapter 3). These radical architectural changes (and their more important cognitive counterparts) would not have surfaced without his on-site perspectives. He was also able, even after fifty years, to look over the once familiar countryside and describe buildings on his farm of which there is no trace today. The construction dates of still other buildings, known to have existed, could be partially verified by the informant's not being able to recall them; that is, they were built after he moved out. He could scan a hillside covered with trees and recount how it was cleared half a century before at ten dollars an acre. It would take four men a week to cut the trees, snake them down the hill, and burn the stumps and underbrush. They would then split the proceeds. As we drove up the third branch, he saw houses of which nothing remains today, nor had there been any recollection of them by younger informants. At one site, as I attempted to visualize the house he had just described, all he could see was himself as a young man, one afternoon fifty years ago, stumbling up the path after too much whiskey.

Yet another informant, returning to the Head for the first time in twenty-five years, shared vivid human images rather than artifactual ones. The simple canning shelves (Fig. 2) in her house evoked deeply personal reminiscences of holding the shelves steady while her father, who died a few years later, nailed them in. She found a multilayered clump of newspaper used to paper the walls, separated it layer by layer until she came to a sheet with a date corresponding to her memory, and held it up, saying, "My mother and I put this paper up together, and here it still is after all these years."[4] Later, as we walked up the hill behind the house to the family graveyard where her father is buried, I counted three chipped rock tombstones and asked who the other two people were. "There are dozens of people buried here," she replied, "all the way up the hillside."[5] The other graves had once been identified by wooden markers, long decayed. Just who was buried there was not within the limits of her memory, nor did she think it was within anyone else's. I knew then, as I stood over the unnamed, that I would never really understand the subtle pattern of life in Hollybush, but only fragmented perceptions. A lifetime of study could not duplicate the knowledge inherent in hoeing corn on the hillside for one day when the Head was a living community.

Since the historical limits of informants' memories were becoming increasingly apparent, it seemed imperative to attempt to piece together the facts about every structure found or mentioned; perhaps an artifactual analysis would reveal what seemed to be otherwise irrecoverable information. And since in a diachronic study the beginning becomes the principal comparative point, controlling questions immediately developed: who was the first person to settle in the Head, when did he do so, and what type of house did he build? Because informants were unsure, I began checking deeds and looking for early settlers' names, but new difficulties arose. Many of the older area deeds described land that had not been surveyed. Organic points like trees and marked rocks had been used to identify boundaries that only the property owners really understood. As more acreage was cleared, these markers vanished. More recent deeds, to land initially surveyed by coal companies, clearly defined property lines; but as they were traced back from grantee to grantor, exact locations again became murky, as this example demonstrates: "A certain tract . . . beginning at the chestnut oak on top of the hill near the rattlesnake den thence running with the top of the hill to the ridge between the waters of Car and the waters of Beaver out to a whiteoak about twenty poles south of the Hollybush Bear wallow thence down Hollybush . . . to include all the patent land the said Franklin owns on said creek 150 acres more or less."[6] Since backward delineation had failed, perhaps reversing tack would produce better results: find who owned all the land first and trace it forward. In a later interview I learned that a Wilson Triplett owned all the land up the right and left Hollybush forks beginning in about 1845,[7] although he domesticated only a relatively small portion of it. Tracing the names of people to whom he sold land meant reinterviewing older informants who could either have been familiar with these people or have heard and recalled family legends about them.

Comparisons of deed descriptions also proved valuable. If no hollows were mentioned in an early deed but were mentioned in later ones, this implied that at the time of the earlier transaction, no one was living in the area to name them. If adjoining properties were not mentioned in boundary descriptions—"beginning at the buck on the right side of Hollybush a conditional line between J.C. Slone and Harvey Caudill"[8]—it was likely that no one was yet living on surrounding sides. A jump in prices from $1.00 to $3.00 an acre in seven years suggested increased settlement during that period.[9] If a hollow's name changed from Rattlesnake Den to Poplar Lick Fork among the same people during a six-year span,[10] there was a possibility that the snakes had been driven out and more attention was being paid to the number of poplars suitable for construction.

As early settlement increased, census records became useful in determining family relationships, birthplaces, occupations (all men were listed as "farmers"), land ownership, property value, and—since the census

information was taken from one family after another in nearly straight sequential order—the relative placement of property and occupants. Determining family relationships gave clues to early settlement patterns. Among the first five adult male settlers in the Head, there were two sets of brothers—John C. and Hardin Slone, and Harvey and Isaac Caudill; John C. and Harvey perhaps enticed their brothers into the area. Also, children often built homes near parents who deeded land to them as inducement to move into or stay in the area.

Another primary census pattern that appeared was the rising expectation of nonagricultural employment. In the 1880 census schedule the question "months not employed" was answered with a check mark made by the census taker next to the occupation of each male head of the household in the Caney Creek area (they answered "farmers" or "farm laborers"), suggesting either full employment or that the question did not apply. By 1900, however, men along Caney still listed their occupations as farmers, but they now tallied the months they were unemployed, averaging about four months per year. It seems possible that they were looking for other types of work than farming and beginning to view agriculture as a secondary occupation to supplement the first. When the logging industry began operating in this area around the turn of the century, for example, a radical shift occurred in the self-awareness of these people as to how they fitted into the overall scheme. Prior to 1900 they lived by what they raised and saw that lifestyle as predominant. In fact, the availability of arable land was the very reason they migrated into the area. After 1900 they viewed the cutting and exporting of local resources as predominant. This cognitive shift paved the way for later acceptance of the promises held out by the renewed discovery and marketing of coal.

As useful as these written sources were, the crucial issue that arose was how well the deeds, references, census records, records of land ownership, and surveyed architecture in the Head of Hollybush corresponded to the oral testimony about the people, their buildings, and their history.

Reconstructing material culture through interviewing has been accomplished previously.[11] However, since some of the building events occurred in Hollybush nearly one hundred years ago and knowledge of them has been passed down only as family history, some corroborative, actual material evidence seemed required.[12] Do the shapes of vanished buildings and the memories of them necessarily correspond? In Hollybush, folk memory did prove accurate when it could be checked against legal documents, the only available written sources.

After the remains of houses were measured and

Figure 3. THE JASPER CAUDILL HOUSE, CIRCA 1950 (courtesy Oliver Caudill).

sketches drawn of their supposed forms, these depictions were shown to informants. On more than one occasion I stood corrected. For example, field notes indicated, from the remains of hewn sills, that one house (No. 14) had been built of log, but three different informants[13] stated that it had been constructed of boards and battens; a recheck of the site revealed, hidden under briars, log piers that could only have supported a house made of light boards, not heavy hewn logs. The foundation stones at another site showed the outline of a saddlebag[14] with 14-by-16-foot rooms (No. 38), yet one informant[15] described the house as a 14-by-14-foot single-pen (No. 13). I told him of my measurements, but he stood by his description. Both the daughter-in-law and granddaughter[16] of the original builder on this site later confirmed the first informant's description, adding that after the builder tore that house down in the early 1930s, two other houses had by turns been put up on the same site. I had found the remains of the last of these three houses. Still another house (No. 20) had been destroyed by fire in 1976, leaving only stone piers and a fallen chimney. After measuring distances separating piers, I showed former occupants,[17] who had lived in the house in the early 1940s, a sketch based on these measurements and on traditional shapes. These informants maintained that not only had a board-and-batten room across the front been left off the sketch, but so had some windows along the wall next to the path. Vansel Slone clearly recalled the windows because he had often sat by the one in the rear kitchen, drinking coffee and looking out at the passersby. A photograph of the house (Fig. 3) was later located in the possession of one of the builder's sons, showing the board-and-batten addition and the windows along the roadside wall. The discrepancy occurred because the log piers supporting the front board-and-batten room had been burned in the fire, eradicating all observable physical evidence of the addition, while the stone piers that had supported the log room and kitchen remained.

A rather sensational example of historical veracity involves the doorway of a single-pen house (No. 7) built in about 1900. Late in this study three informants[18] mentioned the same event, suggesting that the door might be proof of what had occurred. In about 1910, according to family legend, one of the early inhabitants of this house was widowed and then remarried, this time to a much younger woman of whom he was extremely jealous, constantly imagining her unfaithfulness. One afternoon the newlywed man's nephew drank too much alcohol and walked down the path leading to the house, yelling to be allowed in; he climbed onto the porch and began hammering on the front door with his fists. The husband warned him away, saying that if he did not leave, he would be shot right through the door. The young man continued his pounding. The husband, by this time sure this was a suitor to his young wife, raised his shotgun and fired three times through the door, killing the young man. The husband was subsequently tried on a manslaughter charge and spent a year in prison. All three informants mentioned that the shot holes would probably still be in the door, but a check of the photographs I had taken of the house and its door showed only spots of wood rot; a later physical examination of the door showed the same thing. When I asked whether the door had perhaps been removed since the killing, one informant recalled that her father *had* removed the door and placed it over the rear passageway, building a new one for the front.[19] A few days later, while rummaging through the debris of the rear addition, I uncovered a door with three obvious shotgun holes through it. The scattered pellets still rimmed the large, irregular openings. Two were at chest level and one was toward the bottom of the door, the lower blast perhaps misdirected by jangled nerves.

Informants' descriptions of the actual sites of vanished houses proved quite reliable. Many[20] described the positions of three houses[21] I could not locate, but in the early spring, when the apple rose and day lilies

bloomed (as previously noted), I was able to find their remains in the described positions. The existence of one house came to light when an informant casually mentioned that he once lived at the head of the second branch in a single-pen built by Isom L. Slone (No. 10). Although the house has completely vanished, its existence was later substantiated by census records and a coal company deed.[22]

Two informants[23] mentioned a post office in the second branch, operated by John C. Slone in the loft of his large single-pen house (No. 5). Younger informants had little knowledge of the post office and only a vague familiarity with the name John C. Slone. Ellen Hall, however, told of journeying up the main creek path to John C.'s house when she was a young girl in about 1905, recalling that a stairway next to the chimney led up to the post office on the second floor.[24]

However unlikely this seemed, John C.'s application to be postmaster was on record and included a crudely drawn map showing the proposed location of the High Rock Post Office (after the then local name of the second branch) in the Head of Hollybush.[25] Three years later, an application by Isom B. Slone to become the new postmaster and to move the post office to the mouth of Trace also included a map, showing this same location.[26]

Memories of dates of ownership also proved dependable. Two informants placed John B. Slone in the Head in either 1910[27] or 1912.[28] John B.'s deed shows 1910 as the date when he purchased the property.[29] Miles Jacobs was said to have moved into Hollybush and built a house after buying land from Isom L. Slone in about 1925.[30] A deed check showed no such transaction, but it did show that Miles bought land in the described location in 1926 from John D. Slone, Isom L.'s brother[31]—a small error, considering that more than fifty years had passed.

The recalled dimensions of rooms and outbuildings proved accurate to within about one foot. One informant, for example, did not want to venture a guess as to the stall size of his barn. When a figure of 10 feet square was suggested he replied, "Oh no, it was only about 9 foot square."[32] The stalls were, in fact, 9 feet square. Another informant,[33] who had not seen his corncrib in fifty years, described it as being 8 by 12, and 7 feet high, with a 10-foot overhang and a 2-foot-square window. The crib, still standing in 1979, actually measured 7 by 12, and 8 feet high, with a 9-foot overhang and a 1-foot-10-inch-square window.

Interviewing several people helped confirm a floor plan given by any one informant, detailed the changes made in a structure, and clarified its location. Hardin Caudill's house (No. 8) was described by three inform-

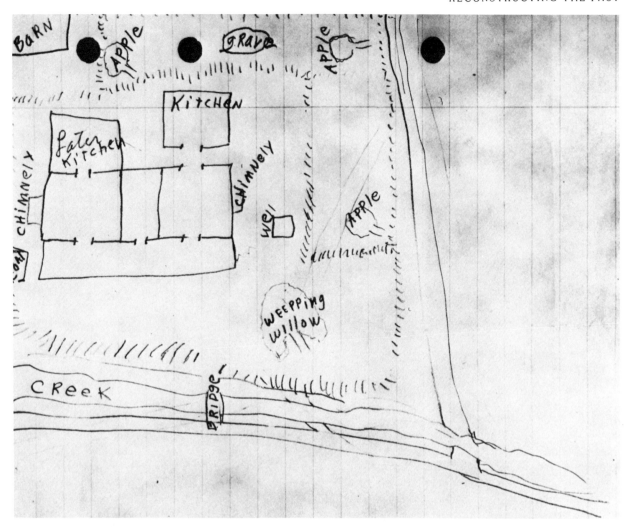

Figure 4. OLLIE CRAFT'S MAP of her grandfather Hardin Caudill's farm, drawn from memory in 1979.

ants as a dogtrot (Fig. 4).[34] Madge Caudill, though, re-membered the house as having had a central chimney. After checking the description with the original infor-mants, I approached Madge again. One image, over sixty years old, helped her correctly recall the chimney's placement: "I remember staying there when I was a little girl. Hardin's wife [Mahala] was tending the fire late at night, and she was sweeping the floor. As I laid there in bed watching her by the firelight, I thought that was an odd thing to do. She should have swept the floor in the daytime, but she was the neatest person I ever knew. I remember her tending the fire, and the chimney *was* on the end of the house, not in the middle."[35]

Only one informant[36] mentioned that Isaac Caudill actually built the house he lived in, constructing it in about 1900. Others, although not positive, thought that Franklin Caudill—Isaac's son—had built the house some years later. The first informant was relying on

family history; description of the exact house site was rooted in the memory of a social visit to that house more than sixty years earlier, when she was a small girl. In support, a 1903 coal company deed noted "a white willow witnessed by the southeast corner of Isaac Caudill's house."[37] The incorporated property descrip-tion was plotted, showing the position of the house in the deed corresponding exactly to the present position of the actual structure. Isaac did build the house some-time between 1893, when he purchased the property,[38] and 1905, when he conveyed it to his son Franklin.[39] In this instance, the informant's recollections clarified facts about the house's builder, position, and approximate date of construction.

Throughout extended interviewing, no informant mentioned a building as having stood in the Head with-out having that fact later substantiated by others and by deeds or census records.[40] Rare discrepancies in de-

Figure 5. TANDY AND ANNA SLONE, CIRCA 1920 (Alice Lloyd College Photographic Archives).

scription occurred in the location of buildings and the treatment of logs (round vs. hewn). In such cases, I generally took the word of the builder over that of an occupant, or valued most highly the word of the person who lived nearest the structure and for the longest time. In one instance, a house was described by two informants who lived out of view of it as having been built of round logs.[41] Another informant,[42] who resided across the creek from the house for twenty years and recalled watching the owner's father instruct others how to hew and notch logs as the house was being erected, described it as hewn. This extra touch, plus his long years just across the creek, made the last informant's description carry more weight.

Still, the longest awaited pieces of information to be collected and substantiated were who the first person was to move into the Head, when, and what type of house he built. In each interview, the question of first settlement was posed, but family history and oral tradition did not seem to extend far enough back. The general response had people living in the Head either one hundred years, 150 years, or before the Civil War, but no specific names or dates were obtainable. Finally, Mary Sparkman, in an interview I thought beforehand would contain little hard information,[43] related a memory of her mother's: as "a young girl," Cynthianne (Mary's mother) had walked in the January snows— behind her father, Tandy Slone (Fig. 5), and in front of the oxen pulling the sled that carried the family's chairs, quilts, featherbeds, clothes, and tools—into the Head of Hollybush for the first time. They traveled from Short Fork over the head of Trace, down to a wide bottom where the first and second branches meet, "and settled about twenty feet from where Isaac Caudill later built his house" in a one-room pole house with a dirt floor and a board roof held in place by weight poles (No. 1). Built the previous fall, its saddle-notched round logs had been gathered when Tandy and some male relatives cut a clearing for the house, the crop (pronounced "crap" by the early settlers), and a few fruit trees. Cynthianne recalled the area as "timber land," meaning—in local usage—unoccupied virgin forest. She had passed on other reminiscences to Mary: cooking took place on a wood fire, and they ate out of shallow depressions chiseled in the flat side of a split log that also served as a table. A bucket of water was sloshed over the "plates" after meals. Clothes were made of wool sheared from the sheep that Tandy later brought into Hollybush. The wool was washed, dried in front of the fireplace, carded, and dyed with walnut bark. "The way they lived is that about everything they had they produced," related Mary. There was no one in the Head then but Tandy, his family, and the animals, both domestic and wild. Bears would often chase the children if they wandered away from the house looking for the milk cows. Once, a search had to be organized for one of Cynthianne's brothers thought to have been carried off by a bear. Actually lost, he was found alive, although he died a few years later of a childhood disease and was buried up on the hillside above the house. When asked how she could be so sure of events that had taken place years before she was born, Mary replied that her mother had told her all about her early life because "I was always a good listener to stories, and I just took it all in as she'd tell it, and I'd always remember it."[44]

If her mother moved into the Head as "a young girl," how did that description translate into actual years? The family Bible lists Cynthianne's year of birth as 1871, and Mary thought the phrase "young girl" described someone about ten to twelve years old. This interpretation would put Tandy Slone's migration into Hollybush sometime between 1881 and 1883. A Floyd County deed records a conveyance from William Triplett, Wilson's son, to Tandy Slone in July 1881.[45] The deed includes land "on the right hand fork of the Hollybush fork of the Caney Fork . . . containing fifty acres in the name of James Hale."[46] Since James Hale had been all through the area in the 1840s, surveying land patents, this particular deed had—miraculously—cardinal points; when plotted, they showed Tandy's land in the Head of Hollybush comprising the bottoms of the first and second branches, meeting where Isaac Caudill would subsequently build his house (Fig. 6). Oral tradition has Tandy migrating into the Head in the early 1880s; both the date and the location are verifiable.

Oral testimony, then, specifically focused on the material artifacts created by individuals in Hollybush, appears reliable when checked against available written or

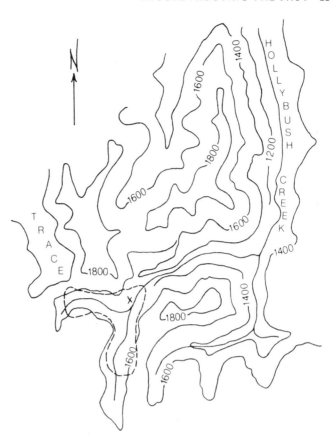

Figure 6. TANDY SLONE'S PROPERTY, PLOTTED FROM HIS DEED. The site of Isaac Caudill's house is marked with an X.

field-checked sources. Certain of Lynwood Montell's conclusions on the trustworthiness of oral history as a historical technique[47] can therefore be modified and applied toward restoring details of material culture now vanished from the landscape:

1. It is necessary to collect multiple descriptions in order to obtain a complete architectural history of a structure. Numerous descriptions tend to confirm rather than contradict each other. A building remains reasonably fixed for long periods and steadily permeates the mind, unlike fleeting events, which may evoke varying impressions among individual witnesses. Differences in description are often accountable to renovations made by different owners with each informant's impressions being fixed on but one era of a building's history. Many sites in the Head of Hollybush had more than one structure built on them. Informants' varying descriptions show not the unreliability of oral testimony, but its completeness in charting changes in what appear to be stable forms.

2. Architectural details are often recalled through

association with incidents, both serious and trivial, that took place in or around the structure in question. One informant recalled[48] details by centering them on images of her father, who died when she was only thirteen: "I helped my father put up those shelves," and "That room had a stone foundation because I remember handing him those flat stones." She remembered barn details by recalling how, after her father died, she had to milk the cow one windy night. She had pulled the cow out of the west stall and was sitting on the stool milking when the strong winds pushed between the round logs and blew out the flame of the coal oil lamp. She continued to sit in the dark, frightened, thirteen years old, wondering what life would be like without her father. Her emotional memories of that night, as well as details of the physical structure that surrounded them, remain crystal clear to this day.

Another informant recalled all details as being before or after June 30, 1940. On that date, after her family had hoed corn all day, they gathered and sat on the porch to cool off. A man who lived with a neighbor up the path and who, as it turned out, had severe mental problems, walked past the house with a shotgun. He stopped, then raised and fired the gun randomly at the family congregated on the porch, killing the informant's brother and wounding her mother and several others. Details of even such things as window placements were tied to that event: she had been lying on the bed sleeping when the gun first went off; she remembered that when she sat up, startled, light was coming through the east wall (No. 19).[49]

Not all recollections tied to artifacts are tragic. Consider the previously mentioned image of Mahala Caudill's sweeping in front of the fire, or that of Boss and Zona Slone who, while unemployed during the summer of 1949, took the time to build a log house (No. 43). The two of them look back fondly on that slow summer when they built their house and ate out of the garden.[50] Mary Sparkman recalled details of a house that Adam Slone built for her grandparents, Tandy and Anna Slone, by associating them with the image she carries of her grandfather walking up the path toward his new home after having been gone for some time in Virginia. His wife, Anna, the informant related,

was a little-bitty delicate woman, all spirit, you know. She was real lively, and when she saw him coming she had the prettiest white apron on, and she went [singing] through the yard, you know, and she made it as she went. She said,

Howdy, howdy-do.
How have you been since I parted from you?
I'll hug you and kiss you and I hope we agree,
And we'll travel on to the sweet Tennessee!

I can remember her singing that when Grandpa came home. [Laughter.] And it was a little log house and she [it] had a little

dug spring. It was walled up with those creek rocks, you know, and I'd go and dip a bucket, and oh, I thought it was all of it to go and dip the water out of that good spring up in the head of that hollow.[51]

The essential descriptive core about Hollybush structures was consistent and agreed with documentation and fieldwork. Some omission of construction details did occur, however. It was difficult for many older informants to recall exact window placement in a house that stood sixty to seventy years ago, yet the floor plans, construction dates, and treatment of materials they did remember could still be used to form an accurate composite visualization.

Specific family legends could be recalled about parents and grandparents but not about great-grandparents, so family history among Hollybush informants was reliable covering events back two generations. Dates, construction sites, and building descriptions were extremely accurate when kept within this generational framework. General family memorates dating first settlement in the Head of Hollybush as sometime "before the Civil War" were of little value when compared to the specific account of Tandy Slone's leading his wife and children in when the informant's mother was "a young girl" and settling where "Isaac Caudill later built his house." This simple fragment of folk history specified a time and place, thereby clearly illuminating the past.

Since numerous descriptions of Head of Hollybush material culture tend to reinforce each other, agree with fieldwork documentation when buildings or their remains still exist, and match written sources as regards dates and sites, oral descriptions of buildings no longer in existence should be regarded as highly accurate. A description of construction techniques must precede an examination of individual buildings, however, in order to provide a creative context for form. As social customs changed in Hollybush, so did the manner in which its shelters were erected. The knowledge of techniques, therefore, will enhance the later accounts of shifting social customs. The act and art of building in Hollybush reflected Hollybush society; a change in one corresponded with a change in the other.

2. Building Techniques

Residents in the Head of Hollybush were, from first settlement to abandonment, responsible for the erection of shelter for themselves and their livestock. Building was not a task deferred to professional architects, building contractors, and mortgage lenders. Rather, the knowledge came internally, by way of tradition and culture, to certain of these people; in their isolated circumstances, they could retrieve this information refined through time and passed down both orally and through observable practice from builder to self-committed observer. What follows is a description of the techniques employed by Head builders and, when known, the rationale behind them.[1]

THE LOG HOUSE. Provisional shelters, called *pole houses* by the first wave of settlers (see Chapter 3, Nos. 1 and 3), varied in construction from later hewn-log houses: because of the structure's temporary intent, workmanship was purposely inferior. The lower wall logs in pole houses, for example, were laid directly on the ground or in shallow trenches. Crudely saddle-notched round-log walls were then stacked—all the way up to the ridge line on the gable ends—and held in place by being notched into the purlins, or the poles supporting the board roof. Since nails were scarce, the roof boards were held down by narrow "weight poles" stretched from gable to gable. The lower weight poles were held in place by being notched into end logs purposely extended out past the walls. Splits of oak, left over after riving the roof boards, were jammed between poles, preventing the higher ones from rolling down (Fig. 7). On occasion, stones were placed on the boards to hold them in place.

The chimney, with a rectangular base and a rounded stack, was made of creek-bed rocks mortared with mud and pebbles. The firebox was large enough for cooking and for accommodating a back log, the one used to bank the fire overnight. The floor was tamped dirt; the door, riven battens. No windows were installed.

Sturdier *hewn-log houses* were usually built within one or two years, providing more durable shelter and implying the intended permanent residence of the builder. Sites for hewn structures were chosen on the basis of good sun and nearby water, either from the creek or from a spring believed to run year round. Builders also wanted to face the people coming toward them or going past. Austin Slone explained the logic of his grandfather's house position (No. 4):

> The road come up there on the other side of the hill, up and down Trace, so we could see people pass. We'd set on the porch when we didn't have nothing to do, and when we'd take a break, you know, working around in the garden or something. Back then, most people had great big porches. They've started narrowing them down now, but they liked them big porches back then. I did. So we'd sit there, and we'd see these people pass, and they passed not too often.[2]

Hewn-log houses were almost always supported by rock foundations, or piers, whose stones often required splitting to achieve the appropriate square or rectangular shape. The stone was first marked with a narrow-point chisel run alongside a square positioned perpendicular to the grain. A larger splitting chisel was then hammered along this visible line. Once an opening was made, iron wedges were driven in to split the stone to shape. These rocks would then fit snugly one over the

17

Figure 7. A WEIGHT-POLE ROOF on a hewn-log house in Knott County, circa 1890 (Alice Lloyd College Photographic Archives).

other in the four cornerstone positions. Some builders thought it necessary to dig about 18 inches below ground level, or below the frost line, in order to avoid having the base stone crumble as a result of temperature variations. Other builders thought it necessary only to dig down to more solid dirt, preferably clay. Still others simply put the foundation stones directly on the ground and compensated for any sinking by inserting chocks between the top stone and the log sill. It was necessary that the foundation stones be laid high enough to get the house 1½ to 2 feet above ground, though, so that air could circulate under the house, preventing excessive dampness from rotting the sills, sleepers, and floorboards. A nonlevel hillside building site could be corrected by piling stones higher in the downhill corners.

The stone piers were positioned to approximate the size of the intended log rooms, which were built large enough to accommodate the particular family and its activities. The spatial rule of thumb was that three beds should fit along the walls away from the fireplace, leaving enough room to gather chairs around the fire and be

able to walk behind them. This walkway's width differed among builders, since room sizes varied from 20 by 24 feet to 14 by 14 feet. Rear additions, normally about 10 feet wide, were calculated on the space needed to house a long table, chairs on both sides, and room to walk behind them.

Once the size was formulated, the stones needed to be set in an absolutely square or rectangular pattern. Two methods were used: measuring the diagonals, and squaring the corners by the 6-8-10 formula. The first was simply a matter of making sure the two diagonal measurements were the same length—22½ feet for a 16-by-16 foot room, for example, or 24 feet for a room 16 by 18 feet—so that the corners would all be 90 degrees. Foundation stones were moved until equal diagonal distances were achieved.

The 6-8-10 method squared a room by measuring 6 and 8 feet from the same corner toward adjacent ones. When the distance from the end of the 6-foot length to the end of the 8-foot length was 10 feet, following the Pythagorean theorem ($A^2 + B^2 = C^2$ on a right triangle), a 90-degree angle was reached (Fig. 8).

Strings were stretched from corner to corner, and the process repeated until the foundation stones were properly aligned.

By the 1920s, commercial cloth tape measures were replacing the older spread-hands method, where the basic unit of measurement was the distance from little finger to little finger. In one variant, the fingers were spread palm down with the tip of one thumb covering the thumbnail of the other. Another variant was to spread the fingers and have the tip of one thumb rest level with the lower joint of the other. A builder marked off his measurements by walking along, continually laying his spread hands down, and counting how many times it was necessary to do so to cover the required distance. This number was then applied to whatever he was fashioning to fit between those two points. Considering the method, distances were said to have been very accurately calculated.

Once the cornerstones were squarely set, the logs could go up. Trees, cut from the surrounding hills with crosscut saws, were picked on the basis of wood type, straightness, and how clear they were of knots. If a felled tree was found to have too many knots, it was left to rot. Those deemed acceptable were pulled down to the site by mule, a process called "snaking." The steep hillsides made it necessary to fasten large chains around the top section of a tree to "grab" the slope and keep the log from sliding down by its own weight. Limbs left on the tree were not enough to slow it down.[3]

Oak or chestnut was used for the sills (the bottom logs) because they could support the weight of the log walls without too much sagging in the often unsupported center. For a rectangular house, the long sills

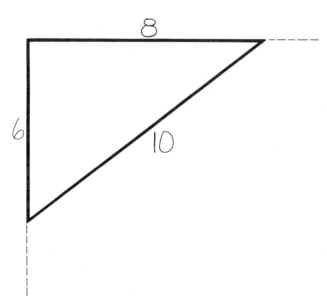

Figure 8. THE 6-8-10 SQUARE CORNER.

were usually square-notched on the ends, placed on the cornerstones (Fig. 9), and leveled—often by eye. The sill was shaped usually on only three sides: top, bottom, and outside edges; the interior edge was hidden by the floorboards. The sills were joined by overlapping the long sill over the short sill or by square notching. Pegs were sometimes driven down through the corners, holding the sills fast.

An articulated advantage to using hewn logs for the walls instead of the more naturally shaped round ones was that water was thought to collect in the outer layers of round logs (called the "sap"), causing them to rot more quickly. When a log was hewn—cut from a round to a rectangular shape—the sap was cut away, and the denser heartwood was believed to repel the moisture. As one informant phrased it, "The hewing does about the same thing as planing your lumber—it smooths it till the water sheds all off."[4]

Part of the reason for the aesthetic value of the shaped logs was the obvious time spent in working them to their final, harshly geometric form. In fact, a hewn-log dwelling was called a house, whereas a round-log dwelling was called a cabin. One builder who made this distinction, however, and who built a cabin as late as 1949, added the contention that round logs would last as long as hewn ones if the roof overhung the walls enough to keep the rain off.[5]

Yellow poplar was normally used for the walls because it was durable and easily shaped with bladed tools. As the poplar was sold to lumber merchants, other trees—oak, chestnut, and even pine—were used, even though some (the hardwoods) were harder to work. After being snaked to the site, the logs were cut with a crosscut saw to the desired length. Two parallel lines, usually 5 to 7 inches apart along the top of the log, were then marked with a long string run through either pokeberry juice or (when coal began being used as fuel) coal soot. The coated string was stretched taut along the log and plunked, leaving visible guidelines. An ax was then used to cut perpendicularly into each side of the log at intervals, up to the line on top. A broadax, swung nearly parallel to the length of the log, was then used to cut away or "hew" the scored wood, leaving a long log flattened on the inner and outer sides. In the early days, the tops and bottoms were hewn flat; later, they were most often left round, with the bark remaining. If a log was wide enough, it was split down the center with dogwood or oak wedges, called "gluts," and hewn on the outside edge; these often measured 20 inches high by 6 inches thick.

The timbers were stacked, alternating end logs with the side logs, and joined by half-dovetailed notching (see Fig. 16),[6] although it was not called that. There were two names in the Head for a half-dovetail notch: a

Figure 9. A SQUARE-NOTCHED SILL ON SHAPED CORNERSTONES.

scribe notch, because the projected shape was "scribed" (or marked) with a sharp object or pencil, and a square notch, because the bottom was square. The reasons given for its use were that besides preventing the logs from pulling apart, its angles pointed down and out, allowing no moisture to run into the notch to collect there and rot the log, and warming sunlight was believed to draw moisture out of the notch after a rain. The saddle notch, the only other type found in the Head (and used in round-log houses), was based on the same principle. Known only as a "notch," it was cut out of the bottom of the log so that moisture ran down and was not allowed to collect and cause decay.

As the level of logs rose, so did the difficulty of lifting them to the required height. Skinned poles were angled between the then top log and the ground so that the remaining logs could be pulled with ropes and pushed by hand up the slick incline. If a curved log had to be used, it was put near the top of the wall and inserted curve upward. Gravity and seasoning were thought to eventually pull the curve down; if installed curve downward, the log would eventually pull that side of the house lower than the others, weakening the entire structure. All interstices between logs were filled in with a mixture of mud and pebbles.

The plates, the top logs on both long sides, were often larger and allowed to overhang the rest of the wall by resting on, or by being pegged or square-notched into, the top gable-end logs, which were extended for support purposes (see Fig. 97). A common explanation given for overhanging the plate (also called the "wall" log) was that it protected the lower wall from damaging rains. Many builders, however, seemed to ignore this line of reasoning by simply making the plate the same size as the rest of the logs and not overhanging it.

Sleepers, or floor joists, were made from oak or chestnut rather than poplar or pine, since they would better support weight. They were fitted in after the walls were up by square-notching the ends, flattening the tops, and angling them into the spaces between the first and second long wall logs. After insertion they were spread out at 15-inch to 2-foot intervals, depending on the builder. Some sleepers were pegged into the sills, but most were not; the floorboards, pegged or nailed into the sleepers, held them in position.

The point at which the floor was put in depended on individual preference: some builders wanted the roof on first to keep out moisture; others put the floor in immediately after the walls were up and the sleepers were set. There were three types of flooring: puncheon, whipsawed, and milled. A puncheon floor was usually made from split poplar logs, about 12 to 18 inches wide, which were smoothed with an adz on the top and bot-

tom surfaces to a 3-inch thickness.[7] Sometimes, though, they were split from oak, smoothed on the top with an adz and drawknife, and flattened on the bottom enough not to rock when set on the sleepers. Whipsawed floorboards were cut with long-bladed two-man saws. One man stood on top of a platform that supported the logs from which the boards were cut, and the other below it, the two sawing out as many as a dozen planks in one session (Fig. 10). Members of the Jacobs family, who lived two miles down the main Hollybush path in Old House Branch, made their money from sawing boards around the turn of the century.[8] Many of the floorboards in early houses in the Head were purchased from them. Beginning about 1915, however, milled floorboards were cut at area sawmills from logs hauled to the mill by the builder. Oak, poplar, and hickory were the preferred woods, but pine and sugar maple were used if necessary. A one-inch thickness was believed to make a sturdy floor, but if the lumber was green, it would curl up on the ends. Often, a second floor was added to keep the first one flat. Tongue-and-groove flooring was not used until after World War II, when it was commercially produced.

The older puncheon and whipsawed floors were fastened by augering ¾-inch holes through the floorboards and about 5 inches into the sleepers. A ¾-inch-square hickory peg, about 7 inches long, was then hammered into each hole to hold the board fast. Since both hole and peg had roughly the same diameter, the floorboard would not split when the peg was inserted, but the square shape of the peg meant it would never loosen.

The next step in construction was the roof. First, the angle of pitch needed to be chosen, but many builders had no formula except to say the roof should be steep enough to shed water. One informant said, "They [builders] just got out and took them two poles [rafters] and cut a notch up there and said, 'That's the way I want it.' "[9] Another informant described this technique in more detail:

We'd fix rafters, you know. Well, one would get up there and hold them together [over an end wall], then we'd get off and look at them, see about what kind of slope we wanted them. There wasn't any certain measurement, only just eyeball it, where it looked like it was steep enough to shed water good. Then after we'd done that, I'd mark them where I told them I thought that was good enough. Then we'd saw them two by them pencil marks there, where they was marked, where they had been held up, and cut the other ones by them.[10]

Even sighting by eye they arrived at something very close to either a 45-degree or 27-degree roof pitch. Some builders used one of two common carpentry

Figure 10. WHIPSAWING BOARDS, CIRCA 1880 (Alice Lloyd College Photographic Archives).

formulas to fix these angles: the 12/12 or 6/12 method (Fig. 11). In the first, a carpenter's square was tilted so that an invisible line connecting the two 12-inch marks was parallel with the ground. This triangle served as a sight against which the roof joists were joined to give them a 45-degree pitch; they were fastened at the top

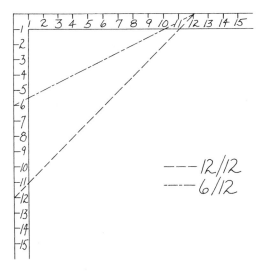

Figure 11. 12/12 AND 6/12 ROOF ANGLES.

with a peg or nail, and then secured to the plates. A string stretched from one apex to the other served as a guide with which to position the other rafters. The second method was to mark the square on the 6-inch and 12-inch lines, tilt the ruler, and use it as a sight to set the joists at about a 27-degree pitch. The 45-degree roof was thought to shed water better because the steeper pitch made it more difficult for rain to blow under the shingles in a strong horizontal wind. As tin roofs became popular after 1945, however, builders realized that the shallower the pitch, the less the square footage, and the more money they could save on tin; and since tin was more watertight, the steeper pitch was less important.

Prior to 1945, wooden shingles, or "boards," were used exclusively as roofing material. White oak was the favored wood for boards, since it was believed to resist moisture longer than any other variety of straight splitting oak—lasting anywhere from twenty-five to fifty years. White oaks became rare throughout the county when tree merchants began using them for making barrel staves. The next choices were chestnut oak and yellow oak. When these water-resistant woods were no longer available, then any other oak was used.

The boards, split out of tree sections with a froe, were 6 to 8 inches wide, 2½ to 3 feet long and ½ to ¾ inch thick.[11] These were then nailed in a double layer onto parallel lathing strips, beginning at the eave. After the first row was in place, either a long board was tacked or a soot-covered string was stretched and snapped across the row about 2 feet from the bottom edge, leaving a visible line. The next row overlapped the first to this line, creating uniform edges considered to look correct (Fig. 12). The marker was moved up another 2 feet and the process repeated up the roof from one eave and then from the other. Since the early pole houses had had their roof boards fastened with poles and sometimes rocks, a properly fastened roof must have had its appeal.

The boards on one side were purposely extended 4 to 6 inches past the other at the ridgepole serving as a rain break to prevent rainwater from leaking into the house through the ridge. In most regions, this slight extension faces the predominantly western winds, also the direction of incoming weather. In the Head, however, weather usually moves up the winding hollows, so the overlap faced out.

The open gables were enclosed with boards cut longer than roofing shingles and attached either vertically or horizontally. Vertically, the boards were fastened to horizontal poles, starting at the gable bottom, with the next row overlapping about 6 inches to shed rain down the oak grain. Horizontally, they approximated clapboarding, with each successively higher board overlapping the lower one by about an inch.

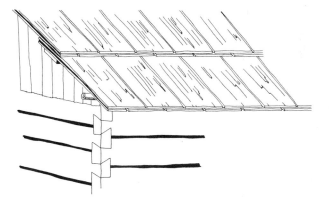

Figure 12. THE BOARD ROOF.

Ceiling joists, made first of round poles and later of milled lumber, were extended across the width of the room at about 2-foot intervals, 7 feet above floor level, and were held in place by either flattening the ends and fitting them into spaces between the logs or by nailing a long board into a log under the pole ends. No special wood type was used. The poles were occasionally shaved flat on the bottom side so that the ceiling boards would fit flush. Froed or riven boards, 4 to 6 inches wide and about 2 feet long, were usually then nailed to the undersides of the poles; obviously, such a ceiling could not have supported human weight. Later, milled boards, similarly nailed to poles, were used for ceilings.[12]

Although a doorway was sawed out of the front wall early on, allowing builders to move in and out, the remaining door, window, and chimney openings were fashioned after the house had been essentially completed; nearly all piercings were central.[13] Framing boards were pegged or nailed against the cut log edges of the door and chimney openings for stability (Fig. 13).[14] Batten doors were positioned in the long walls;

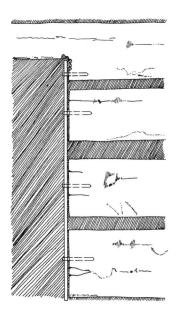

Figure 13. A STABILIZED FIREPLACE OPENING.

they were made of split or milled boards, pegged or nailed to three equally spaced horizontal braces that faced into the room, making the door almost impossible to kick apart from the outside. All doors swung in, but neither left- nor right-hand openings seemed favored. Window openings were originally covered with batten shutters, but these were replaced by glass when it became available. The earliest glass windows were permanently fixed and could not be opened. In the 1920s, Green Slone began making sash windows—two panes in each sash—for his neighbors, using a rabbet plane (called a "molding" plane locally). By the mid-1930s other builders were also fashioning their own windows with glass and putty purchased in the county seat and

sashes planed at home.[15] Occasionally, windows were set in sideways,[16] increasing horizontal visibility and reducing the number of logs that needed to be cut out of a wall to provide an opening.

The last step in construction was the chimney. Space for the lower chimney was almost always cut out of a gable wall, with the stack built up outside the wall from the shoulder. The base of the chimney was always rectangular, and its size depended on whether wood or coal was the intended fuel. A wood fireplace required a width of about 6 feet and a depth of 4 feet to accommodate a 4-foot-wide by 2½- to 3-foot-deep firebox. A coal-burning fireplace needed to be only 3½ feet wide by 2½ feet deep for a 2- to 2½-foot-wide by 1- to 1½-foot-deep firebox. A chimney extending no less than two feet above the ridgepole encircling a 12-inch opening was the size most often mentioned for a properly drawing fireplace, even one that served two fireboxes.

Stones came from either the field and creek or what were called "rock quarries." One type of quarry was in substratum sandstone where moisture had separated the horizontal sedimentary layers. This thin stone was used in many of the older and larger chimneys. The layers broke cleanly from each other and could be easily shaped with a dull ax or mattock into the desired rectangular shape. Larger chimney stones were cut from sandstone quarries above ground level. Hammers, point chisels, and rock chisels were used to mark and split the stone into the proper shape, usually about 16 by 8 by 6 inches. Field and creek-bed stones were of assorted sizes and were usually left unshaped.

After the chosen rock type had been hauled to the site in a corn sled, the foundation was laid, either below the frost line, on solid clay below the topsoil, or on large embedded rocks secure enough to hold the proposed chimney upright. Field and creek stones, laid in rough courses, were mortared with clay. Blue or white clay, mixed with a little water, was a favorite because chimney heat baked it into a durable bonding material. Often small pebbles or pieces of coal were added to lesser grade clays to make them more stable. Thin quarry rock was laid in a stretcher bond without mortar. Quarry stones large enough to extend the full width of the chimney (see Fig. 104) were mortared with mud or, after World War II, commercial cement.

The firebox was usually outlined with three long rectangular stones: the horizontal arch rock held up by two vertical jams, often shaped smooth for appearance. The throat leading into the stack was angled only slightly and did not prevent cinders from going directly up and onto the roof. This caused no great concern among builders. Even double chimneys, separated one from the other by a 5-inch partition, had a straight stack

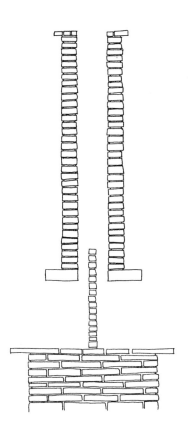

Figure 14. THE DOUBLE-FIREBOX CHIMNEY.

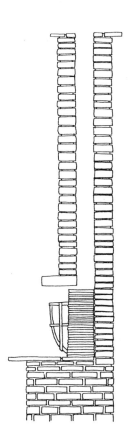

Figure 15. THE SINGLE-FIREBOX CHIMNEY, with backroll and coal grate.

(Fig. 14). Occasionally, the concern that smoke might come back down the chimney caused builders to install smoke shelves—stones jutting out into the stack in an alternating pattern—a system said to have had limited success. Tin, from either of two sources—five-gallon lard cans or washtubs—was used as flashing material, jammed between chimney stones and sealed with mud above and below.

When a wood-burning fireplace was altered to burn coal, the back and sides of the firebox were narrowed with thin pieces of shaped sandstone. A 2- to 3-inch space was left open between the bottom of the arch rock and the top of this new enclosure, known locally as a "backroll." A coal grate was then attached to the backroll with stiff wire inserted between stones (Fig. 15). A coal fire was thought to draw best through this narrow space; also, the heat from the grate was thrown out into the room, not wasted by going up the stack. Fireplaces originally intended to burn coal were built shallow and thus did not require a deep backroll to force heat out into the room. Unlike wood-burning fireplaces, the smaller coal fireplaces were not used for cooking because by that time there was increased acceptance of the cookstove.

Once a house was completed, builders frequently added three-walled rooms to existing four-walled homes, either by spiking the open log ends to already standing corners[17] or by nailing the logs to supporting interior posts (Fig. 16). In one instance,[18] hewn open ends were joined onto an older dwelling by first augering and then chiseling squared areas out of two of the house's dovetailed corners and the log ends of the new room. After inserting these ends into the notches, they were secured with iron spikes (Figs. 17 and 18).

The technology employed to build a *round-log house* was similar to that used for hewn. Differences lay in the overall treatment of the wall logs. Where hewn logs were carefully shaped, all the bark was left on round logs; they were merely trimmed of their branches and saddle-notched at the ends. The plates were usually left round but were occasionally squared and set into a wall with the long hewn sides either parallel or perpendicular to the ground.[19] They never overhung the walls, however.

A round-log house decayed quickly if not protected by long, overhanging eaves; moisture would collect under the bark and between the logs where surface tension carried the water. Although some builders be-

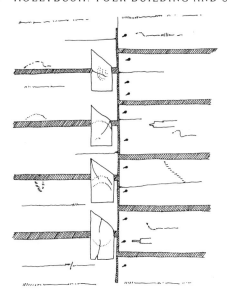

Figure 16. A NAILED THREE-WALLED-ROOM LINK. The addition (right) is attached to an interior post.

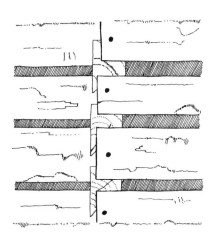

Figure 17. A PEGGED THREE-WALLED-ROOM LINK. The addition (left) is attached to a half-dovetail-notched corner.

lieved that round logs would last as long as hewn ones, they actually did not. When the roofing material on Tom Caudill's house (No. 19) was removed for use elsewhere, both rooms—the hewn and the round— were simultaneously opened to the elements; thereafter, the round-log room, twenty to twenty-five years younger, decayed far faster than the hewn one. A round-log house did require less work and less time to erect, since its logs did not require hewing and elaborate notching, but a builder who believed a round-log house

would last as long as a hewn one was mistaken. When round-log houses became more popular in the 1930s, though, the builders' definition of longevity had changed; a house that survived twenty to thirty years was considered as lasting long enough.

THE BOARD-AND-BATTEN HOUSE. The last type of house built in the Head was constructed of boards and battens, usually assembled without framing studs. Whereas a frame house is supported by a skeletal structure independent of the wall coverings, a "box" house (the regional name for a board-and-batten structure) is not. If the wall coverings of a frame house, both interior and exterior, are torn down, the house will continue to stand. In box structures, the walls are the critical components; if they are removed, the structure will collapse.[20]

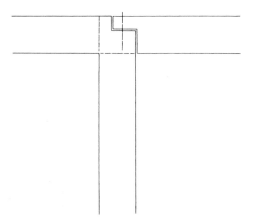

Figure 18. OVERHEAD VIEW OF PEGGED LINK.

The box floor plan and dimensions normally resembled those of either single-pen or saddlebag log houses. However, unlike the log house, a box house could be constructed quickly by two or three men; the material was lighter and easier to handle, and did not require the skill needed to shape logs or to fashion notches. The box-house builder, rather than cutting logs to length, had boards cut to height, since they were assembled vertically instead of horizontally. After the order was filled at a local sawmill, the boards were hauled back into the Head by corn sled, and any miscalculations in length were later corrected with a handsaw.

Once the site was chosen and the house's cardinal position decided upon, either a stone or log foundation was built for it. Stones were split the same way as for the log house. Since the weight of the box house was less, though, the stones did not need to be set as deep. This lighter weight also meant that log piers could be used. Durable hardwoods like oak or beech, at least a foot in diameter, were cut into approximately 2-foot lengths and each one set on end on a flat stone, keeping ground moisture away and slowing decay. In some cases, stones were used under house corners and log piers at midwall.

Sills were usually made of hewn poplar; poplar was not as sturdy as oak, but heavy, sagging walls were not a problem in a box house. Pegs or long iron spikes were often used to secure the square-notched sill ends together (Fig. 19A), and when a log pier was used, they were driven down into it for added stability. The sleepers, made from either oak logs flattened on top or milled two-by-sixes, were notched onto the sills and covered with a milled-board floor. Since the floorboards were usually green, another floor was nailed over it to retard curling. If the house was intended to be a saddlebag, a space large enough to accommodate the double fireplace near the center of the structure was not floored.

Corner posts were erected next by taking two 1-by-12-inch planks, 8 feet in length, and nailing them vertically into a sill corner, overlapping them on the ends for added strength. Since there was nothing on top to which to fasten the corner posts, they required temporary bracing. Once this process had been repeated on the other three corners, 2-by-8-inch planks, spliced and braced in places because of the long spans, were stretched from corner-post top to corner-post top (Fig. 19B) to serve as plates and fastened with nails. This frame could not be considered weight supporting, but together with the sills it gave upper and lower points to which boards and battens could be attached.

The 1-by-12-inch boards and the 1-by-4-inch battens (known locally as "strips") acted as both walls and weight-bearing supports. First an 8-foot-long board was set in vertically, flush against any corner-post board, and nailed into the sill and the milled plate. This was repeated along the projected four walls of the house. A batten was then nailed over each opening between boards to prevent horizontal movement and to slow the tide of wind and weather invading the house.

After the walls were up, more 2-by-8-inch boards, now used as ceiling joists, were square-notched on the ends, stretched across the width of the house from plate to plate at about 2-foot intervals, and nailed in place (Fig. 19C). Ceiling boards were temporarily laid on top of the joists under the proposed ridge line so that a person could stand on them and position either milled-board or pole rafters. When the rafters and lathing were in place (Figs. 19D and E), a board or tin roof was fastened on. Care was taken to overlap the gables and walls by about 1½ feet, helping to keep them dry. Once the roof was in place, the ceiling boards were nailed to the joist bottoms.

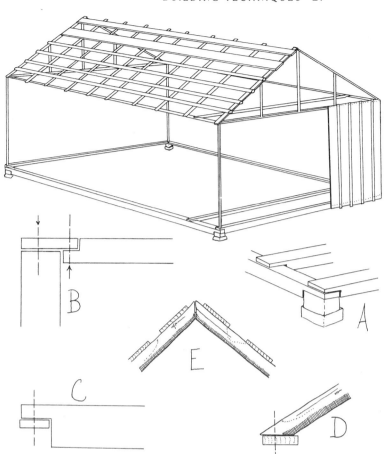

Figure 19. THE BOX HOUSE: (A) notched sills and sleepers; (B) the plate-cornerpost assembly; (C) a ceiling joist notched onto the plate; (D) a rafter and plate; (E) the rafters with board lath.

Interior partitions were constructed by first nailing boards onto the floor and ceiling, directly above and below where the walls were to go. Vertical planks were then nailed into both boards; no battens were necessary. (Occasionally a partition extended down through the floorboards, meaning that it was installed before the floor was laid.)

Door and window openings were symmetrically positioned as the house neared completion. All doors were central to either the room or the front wall they pierced; all windows were set centrally in the wall or between the door and nearest wall. In one case, the vertical 2-by-4-inch boards used to frame the doors and windows were purposely extended from plate to sill, adding structural stability to the walls.[21]

Doors were made of milled battens and were built like those in log houses; the windows were generally sash. The last step, the chimney, followed the methods previously discussed. *All* box houses, however, had the smaller coal-burning fireboxes. As a form of insulation, all interior walls and ceilings were covered first with cardboard (obtained free from storekeepers who saved cartons for this purpose) and then with newspaper, catalog, or magazine pages.

DECORATION. The desire for decoration in folk architecture is frequently expressed by the inclusion of such decorative devices as Gothic trim, decorated cornices, beaded siding, and wainscot. These do not alter the structural strength of the building, but they do help add a sense of visual pleasure to the necessity of providing shelter. In the Head of Hollybush none of these visual reliefs was present; perhaps the aesthetics of a well-shaped hewn log supplanted the desire to decorate woodwork. Still, there was an evident impulse to individualize, to personalize, and to decorate. Boss Slone explained that when he built the chimney in his first house (No. 33), he rounded the top of the stack because, to him, "it was prettier that way, nicer to look at."[22] The log fronts of other houses were covered with boards and battens because they were thought to make the house look more fashionable. Builders considered new or freshly painted roof tins extremely attractive,[23] and almost all houses had either day lilies, apple rose, tulips, or roses planted somewhere close by.

But the most far-reaching decorative method, in terms of wide appeal and individualization, was the papering of interior walls with newspapers, catalogs, magazines, or any combination of the three—a practice stretching back in the area for at least eighty years[24] and the norm for two critical reasons; there was a lack of cash for paint (commercial wallpaper did not become readily available in this area until the 1940s), and the paper served as insulation against the weather, which invaded the house through the small cracks and openings that formed between the logs and chinking or between the boards and battens.

By and large the province of women, the application and placement of media pages was highly structured and followed collectively established patterns, but still allowed for the possibility of individualized expression. Most important, this practice was based on the Appalachian custom of transforming nonfunctioning machine-made objects into objects fit for everyday use. Worn-out shoes, for example, became hinges, and empty lard buckets were turned into stools as well as chimney flashing.

A log wall first had to be prepared for papering, however, by applying a heavy paper or cardboard to smooth out uneven surfaces and by filling any large holes with wads of rolled paper or burlap, since the wallpaper would split over any open spaces as the paste dried. Children also had a tendency to want to stick their fingers through such places, and proper applica-

tion meant that no tears or breaks could appear. A box house had straighter walls and did not need as much preparation—only a cardboard underlining.

Paper saved for wall covering was held on with a boiled flour-and-water paste, which, when mixed to the right consistency, was thin enough to spread evenly but too thick to run down the walls. It was important to remove the lumps either by hand or with a short broom. One former paperer recalled: "You take your hand and get all the lumps out of it. Then you stir it and it will be very smooth. If it lumps, it's not very good. It's not good to leave it over either. You usually try to use up what paste you make that day or it's not very good."[25] A paste mixed so that it was smooth and clear would not show through the paper. Red pepper and rat poison were sometimes added to keep the mice from eating it. The dried roots of sweet anise and arrowroot, after being ground to a fine powder, were also stirred in to give the paste a sweet aroma. The act of papering itself was thought to give a room a fresh look and smell.

The sheets were laid flat on a table, and a small amount of paste was dabbed in the corners, around the edges, and once or twice in the center with a small brush. It was then applied to the wall, beginning in any corner. The next sheet overlapped the previous page by about an inch, and particular attention was paid to keeping the borders straight. Straight edges were thought to look correct; if the lines were not uniform, a papered wall could not be considered attractive. Either of two basic patterns of application, horizontal or vertical, was followed. Any pages that overlapped the edges of the wall were carefully trimmed with scissors or pocketknife.

Of the three types of paper used, magazine paper was the favorite, partly because of its heavy weight and durability. Newsprint and catalog pages were lighter and needed to be papered over as often as every two weeks because they discolored easily. One informant told of her father's remark that he needed to rush home before the dress styles in the paper pasted to the walls changed again.[26] Newspaper did have its advantages, though: if sheets without photographs were chosen, it was thought to approximate a wall painted white, and the dominant white background was the reason for using only newspaper on ceilings. Before electricity, it reflected outside light better and made the room seem brighter. Also, stray pages with photographs were thought to upset the visual uniformity of a wall or ceiling. Pages with photos, on the other hand, were sometimes consistently chosen so that the wall was awash with what were considered interesting images. A policy in favor of photo or nonphoto pages was flexible enough to change, however, by the next papering.

In general, it was thought important that the print be

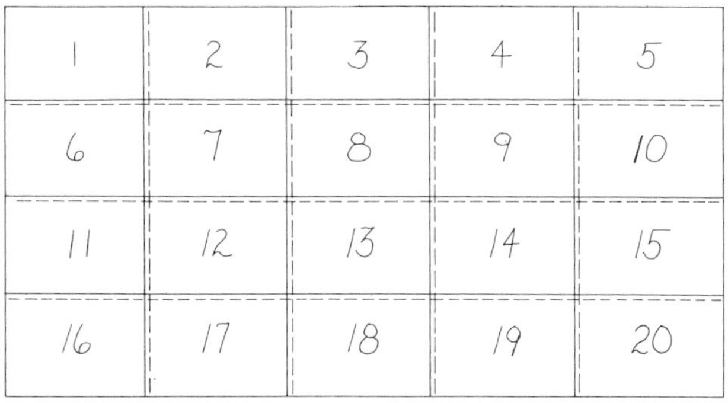

1	2	3	4	5
6	7	8	9	10
11	12	13	14	15
16	17	18	19	20

Figure 20. A NEWSPAPERED WALL DIAGRAM: one possible sequence of application.

right side up, but the older, illiterate residents could often tell direction only by the inclusion of pages with photos. These they evenly spaced with nonphoto pages so that an acceptable mixture ran along the wall. If no photo pages were available, it was still necessary to have the edges absolutely straight, even though the printing was often upside down.

Sometimes, geometric designs were created by cutting the pages square and alternating them so that the printed columns were vertical in square 1 (Fig. 20), for example, horizontal in square 6, vertical in 11, horizontal in 16, horizontal in square 2 . . . and so on to form a checkerboard pattern. A variant had the columns in squares 1, 6, 11, and 16 running vertically and columns in squares 2, 7, 12, and 17 horizontally to give the walls a striped effect. These were called "crazy quilt" walls.

Usually, if not enough of one type of paper was available to go around a room, then two or more types were used—but not on the same wall, because that was thought to be too visually disordered. Newspaper might be used on three walls, but even if there was enough to do half of the fourth, catalog paper, for example, was substituted.

Another use of newsprint was to serve as a bland background for preferred color magazine pictures pasted in the center of a wall or over the fireplace. In this case it was important not to use newspaper with photos, which could detract from the focal point. The outline of the wall was like a large frame, the newsprint the mat, and the magazine picture the painting. Sometimes the central picture was further accented in one of two ways. The newspaper intended for the wall edges could be accordion-folded and notched on one end with scissors. When unfolded, the cut end opened into a symmetrical design which was then pasted along the perimeter of the wall; the darker colored cardboard underneath accentuated the scalloped edges. (This device was used even without benefit of a central picture.) The other mode was to paper the perimeter with random

magazine pages to serve as a contrasting, colorful border to the white background and as an accent to the central picture area.

Each wallpaperer exercised personal preference in her choice of the middle picture. Preferred subjects were Christmas, houses, automobiles, and ornately prepared food dishes. One woman recalled: "I remember in a farm magazine one time when you opened it, it had a picture in the middle. It was a farm, and that was so pretty I remember putting that over the mantel and then putting white around it. It was all different things, farm horses and cattle in this big barn; it was pretty."[27] Another informant liked pictures of flowers because she thought they approximated the still lifes that hung on the walls in homes outside the area.[28] Still another used Norman Rockwell covers from the *Saturday Evening Post* because they "kind of told a little story,"[29] which her small children, who had not yet learned how to read, could appreciate. Some people placed cartoons and Sunday funnies along the lower walls at about eye level for the smaller children, who could then move around the room looking at one after the other. Since the walls were frequently repapered, there was always a fresh round of cartoons.

Newspaper articles that mothers wanted their children to read were also pasted up. Two informants told how they learned to spell "Cincinnati" from articles, and another said all her children learned the alphabet by playing a game where one of them would sight a letter on the wall and the rest would try to locate it by following his announcements as to whether they were getting closer to it or farther away. Variants of this game were played with colors and subjects on the magazine and catalog pages.

Meredith Slone said she made a special point to paste newspaper poems in positions where she could read them while she worked. She learned to do this over sixty years ago as she sat at the table eating with her father. As she tells it:

I learned a many a poem right off the wall when I was a little girl. Me and my dad learned poems off the wall when I was nine years old. It was right up over the table where we ate, and he told me, "Let's me and you see which one can remember this the longest," and he's been dead about ten years. He remembered it the last time I talked to him, and I remember it, too. It tickled me and him. It said,

Foxes could talk if you know how to listen,
   Pa said so.
Owls have big eyes that sparkle and glisten,
   Pa said so.
And bears can turn flipflops and climb big elm trees and steal all the honey away from your bees and they don't mind the winter because they never freeze,
   Pa said so.

Girls is scared of a snake, boys ain't,
    Pa said so.
Girls run and holler and sometimes they faint,
    Pa said so.
A boy'd be ashamed to be frightened that way when
all a snake wants to do is play. You've got to believe
every word that I say,
    Pa said so.
They're as fond of a game as they are of a fight,
    Pa said so.
Most all the animals found in the woods ain't
all time fierce, most time they're good. The
trouble is mostly they're misunderstood because,
    Pa said so.

[*Laughter.*] Ain't it funny? One thing that made me remember it so good was me and him saying let's see which one can remember it the longest. The last time I talked to him not long before he died, he asked me if I remembered it and I said yes, and he said he did too and he said it to me.[30]

Magazine paper did not need to be changed as often as newspaper. One informant noted: "When I could get a *Life* or a *Post* [*The Saturday Evening Post*] or something, why they were the most precious ever was, and we'd save them, you know. I'd use them and they'd last maybe a year and they'd stay white, but newspaper you'd have to paper every two weeks because they'd turn yellow."[31] Magazine color pages, as previously noted, were especially popular. After the wire staples were removed, the pages were dabbed with paste and advantageously arranged on the wall so that the eye would fall on the images to which the paperer was most attracted. These were the pictures even neighbors would stop and comment on.

Since walls were repapered at least once a year, it gave the paperer the opportunity to find new images reinforcing the same theme, or to change themes entirely, thus showing new personality facets, though sometimes at risk. One informant put a picture of a car in the middle of a wall and recalled that "my sisters laughed at me, made a joke about it because I kept this car in my bedroom on the wall."[32] She later added that she used cars because they represented the means to get to all the places, particularly the cities, she wanted to see.[33]

With magazines, as with catalogs, there was some segregation by subject matter. Pictures of food were pasted on the walls where the family ate and recipes near the stove, visually reinforcing spatial function. Some people arranged magazine pages across from where they slept, not necessarily by subject but by color. At night the light of the coal fire would reflect off the glossy colored walls, causing those special chosen hues to dance as the residents fell asleep.

The third type of paper extensively used came from old Sears, Roebuck and Montgomery Ward catalogs.

Some people pasted up the pages in the order they came from the book. Others, though, saw that method as breaking esoteric rules. For example, some informants never mixed tools with clothes or with shoes; they kept subjects closely related within the same room or picked certain motifs corresponding with room use: toys for boys where the boys slept, girls' dresses in the girls' area, and dresses and shoes in the adults' bedroom. As the paper went up, family members were allowed to pick the subjects that, until the next papering, would define the limits of their individual space. Irene Slone remembered that she liked pictures of furniture:

That is what I would always pick when my mother would be papering mine and my sister's room. I'd pick the pages that had the living room couch and chairs to match and an old rocking chair sitting in the background. And also the bedroom suites, like the bed and the chest and the dresser, and usually you'd see a dog sitting in the background in the corner. I picked things like that. That's what I liked my bedroom to be papered with.[34]

The subjects used in the communal living areas were generally chosen at the discretion of the paperer. One informant expressed an additional rule that papered walls did not go well with linoleum floors, only with wood floors or hooked rugs.[35]

Other types of paper, not as widely utilized as the basic three, were used on the walls for a different effect. Before World War II, paper flour sacks were white on the outside and covered with print, but the inside was colored a robin's egg blue. Women were careful then to open the sack by the folds without tearing it. When the flour had been used, the bottom was also unfolded; the sacks were laid flat and saved until enough had been accumulated to cover a wall. Then all the frayed ends were trimmed with scissors and the sacks applied with continued care concerning straight edges. Some took red paper from other kinds of sacks and outlined the blue wall with it. The red border could also, at the paperer's discretion, be scalloped. After 1945 a heavy, commercially produced blue paper was used, fastened to the walls with round pieces of tin nailed on at two-foot intervals. These tins were used partly because they were said to reflect light in a pleasant manner.

Media paper had other decorative uses: instead of pasting scalloped pieces on the walls, paperers often hung them from the mantel, from the cupboards, along the window sills, and, if visible, from the ceiling joists. One informant, though, when talking about such decoration, expressed how taste and values had changed:

You could cut that [newspaper] out in all kind of little designs, you know. Fold it together and cut it out. Oh, you just learn a lot of things when you have to make your own. But now, you know, it wouldn't go good now, but it was really pretty then. And everybody lived alike, you know, that was the thing about it. Nobody, even if somebody had a little more money, they didn't show it. And now everybody wants to live just a little bit more than somebody else.[36]

These cutouts, called "lacing,"[37] were considered a pretty decoration in themselves, but if the doors and windows were left open on a warm, windy day, they would tremble in the breeze—an additional visual treat usually reserved for springtime.

There were other decorations heralding spring. Shade trees near the house had their trunks whitewashed with a mixture of white clay and water. In the house, the firebox was cleaned of its soot and ashes, and the grate was taken out and scrubbed down to the metal. Orange clay was then rubbed over the front of the grate before setting it back in the firebox. The fireplace arch and jam rocks were coated with white or blue clay, and willows or garden roses were cut, placed in the grate, and allowed to extend out a short distance into the room.

Spring cleaning was even considered a form of decoration. Children were sent down to the creek to pound white sandstone into granules, which were then spread over the poplar floor and rubbed in with a hickory scrub broom until the boards looked white. Mary Sparkman recalled cleaning's joys:

That good fresh smell of clay. There were clay banks, and you'd go and get that and it was already gooey, you know, and it was just white as it could be, and when it would dry, it was as white as snow. A lot of people that didn't want to paper, they would put that over the ceiling. It was just like paint, it was beautiful. And when we scrubbed our floors—we didn't have rugs of any kind—and when we scrubbed our floors, we beat up the whitest sand rocks. That was a day's work for the children to take a hammer and beat up all that sand, if you was going to scrub the next day. We would sprinkle that, after we had rinsed it all off, scrub it and rinse it all off, then we would sprinkle that sand over it and let it lay on there until it dried. Then sweep it off and it was just as white and smelled so good and fresh.[38]

This scrubbing was extended by some people to include the door and window facings, and even the chairs. White or blue paint was sometimes used on the door and facings, although not on the house's exterior. Log and board walls were not considered to take to paint very well; cost was also a factor.

What is left of all this decoration done years ago is the image of a room freshly papered with edges perfectly straight, the floors and doors white, the green of spring extending out from the once black heat source, and the lacing moving sporadically in the breeze that made its way through the opened doors and windows.

One obvious value of these decorations was, of course, thrift: the Head resident could visually improve his surroundings with a minimum of capital. Another was cleanliness: if one walked into a house, however humble, and found clean paper on the walls, the housekeeper was automatically considered to be a good one. A third value was more inclusive: even if only one medium was spread throughout the interior walls of a house, each family member could relate to its varied images on an individual basis. One member might, at any one time, alternately see an image as artistic, educational, entertaining, or related to dreams. Irene Slone recalled pasting pictures of cities in the center of her wall and poetically reasoned "I've never been to a large city in my life, and I'm a little bit like Tom Sawyer. I guess I like to explore. I explore with my mind even if I've never been there."[39]

OUTBUILDINGS. All outbuildings utilized the same construction materials as did houses. They were square or rectangular, made of horizontal log or vertical board walls, with a board or metal roof.

A *barn* was designated as a combination structure which sheltered stock, feed, and equipment,[40] the stock being housed in the lower stall(s), the feed in the upper loft, and the equipment in the aisleway or under the overhang. Logs, both hewn and round, were half-dovetailed, saddle-notched, or both, depending on the origin and treatment of individual logs. Since logs could not always span required distances, lap joints secured with pegs were used. Pole ceiling joists were set between the logs the same way as in houses and covered with weight-supporting riven boards split out in long 6- to 8-foot lengths so they would not to slip down between the joists. Occasionally milled boards were used. The rafters were similar to those used in houses except that they were never supported on overhanging plates. If the barn was made exclusively of round logs, the plates and sills were also left round, as opposed to the hewn plates sometimes used in round-log houses.

Cribs were defined as buildings sheltering agricultural products and were set both high and low off the ground on a rock or pole foundation. A high foundation kept air circulating underneath and excessive moisture away from the lower levels of stored produce. Floors were usually made of unsmoothed, split logs fitted between the lower wall logs and were unsupported by floor joists. These logs were set in with either the round or the flat side up, but the two were never mixed. The lofts were built the same way as in barns. Cribs were sometimes constructed, walls and floors, of long riven boards split from oak or chestnut and fastened with nails to a light pole frame.

Hog Houses were usually built of round logs and followed the techniques used to build log barns and cribs. Occasionally, they included a loft, and a puncheon floor instead of a dirt one.

Chicken Houses were generally built of riven boards nailed to a light pole frame—walls, floor, and roof. Occasionally, milled boards were used for the walls and were applied horizontally.

Smokehouses built prior to 1925 were said to have been constructed of hewn logs, but the more recent ones were box construction with a milled-board floor and tin roof.

Piercings on all outbuildings were usually central. The doors and window shutters were made of riven or milled boards nailed to horizontal bracings,[41] with an occasional diagonal brace replacing the middle one. Whereas house doors opened in, barn and crib doors opened out for added interior space.

Hinges generally were made of horseshoes cut and shaped by a local blacksmith into a curved strap. Other recycled materials used were hinges no longer suitable in the house and leather from old boots. Some outbuildings had harr-hung doors,[42] which were held in place by wooden or metal sockets. Doors were fastened shut with short sections of chain looped over a nail or with slide bar latches. Interior partitions were made of either logs, riven boards, or milled lumber.

Where the house faced the road or the direction of oncoming traffic, the barn and crib faced either the house or the direction of work and were not bound to follow the cardinal direction of the house's ridge line.[43] Chicken houses and smokehouses always faced either the front or kitchen door of the house, discouraging thieves.

Not all building techniques used in the Head of Hollybush existed simultaneously. Rather, many techniques (as well as building materials) were replaced: the shaped log, for example, was superseded by the unshaped log or the milled board in response to the society's need to adapt architecturally to new cultural ways. The architectural component of this transition becomes more evident as the individual buildings are described in the order of their construction.

3. Artifactual Survey of the Head of Hollybush

The following surveyed artifacts[1] have been arranged chronologically in order to demonstrate schematically the architectural patterns and transitions that occurred in Hollybush between settlement in 1881 and abandonment in 1960. Each numbered structure has also been indicated on the building map (Fig. 21), showing artifactual proxemics. The listing of houses and community service buildings is complete. Barns, outbuildings, graveyards, and coal banks—all materially integral to Appalachian farm life—were too numerous for total inclusion; therefore, only representative samples were chosen. In the floorplans that follow, a double line

indicates a log wall; a single line, a box wall; a broken line, the covered porch. If no door is shown, the direction in which it swung is unknown.

In addition to the use of floor plans, all buildings have been described by code (see below) detailing important construction particulars.

For an example of how this code works, see the box below the floor plan of artifact No. 1. Reading from left to right, the code shows this one-room house to have been built in 1881 for Tandy Slone out of round logs (RL), which were saddle-notched (S). The wood type is unknown. The chimney was made of creek rocks (CR),

WALL MATERIAL		NOTCHING		WOOD TYPE		CHIMNEY MATERIAL	
HEWN LOG	HL	HALF DOVETAIL	HD	CHESTNUT	Ch	CREEK ROCK	CR
MILLED BOARD	MB	SADDLE	S	OAK	O	QUARRY ROCK	Q
RIVEN BOARD	RB			PINE	PN	SANDSTONE	
ROUND LOG	RL			POPLAR	P	SLAB	SS

HEAT SOURCE		ROOFING		FLOORING		PRESENT STATUS	
COAL FIREPLACE	C	RIVEN BOARD	RB	DIRT	D	FALLEN	F
COAL STOVE	CS	TAR PAPER	TP	MILLED BOARD	MB	MISSING	M
WOOD FIREPLACE	W	TIN	T	PUNCHEON	P	STANDING	S
				RIVEN BOARD	RB		
				WHIPSAWED BOARD	WB		

A blank box suggests an unknown; a line (——), unapplicable information; an arrow (——➤), eventual transition.

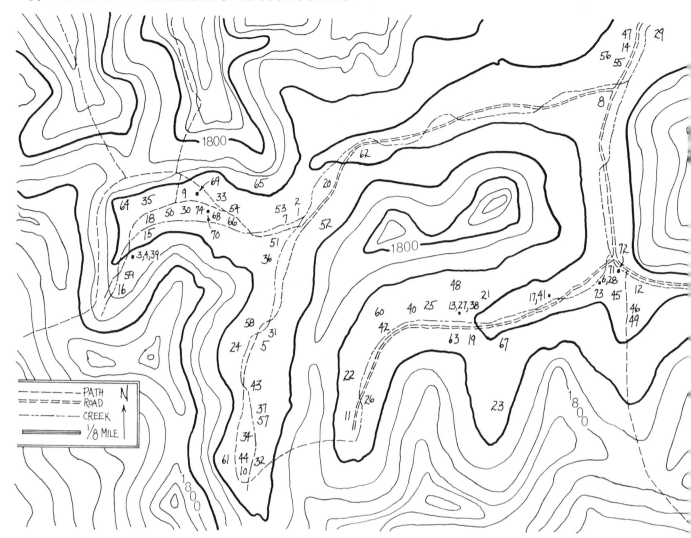

Figure 21. BUILDING MAP OF THE HEAD OF HOLLYBUSH, suggesting the relative geographic positions of numbered artifacts.

incorporating a large wood-burning firebox (W). A riven board roof (RB) protected a tamped dirt floor (D). This structure no longer exists (M).

Artifact No. 4, as another example, shows the development of what was to become a large three-room house. The first room (i) was build between 1887 and 1889 by Adam Slone out of hewn logs (HL) which were half-dovetailed (HD). The wood was poplar (Pr). The chimney was composed of creek rocks (CR), housing a wood-burning firebox (W); a riven board roof (RB) covered the puncheon floor (P). Adam built the second room (ii) between 1900 and 1905, again of hewn, half-dovetailed poplar logs. This time, however, the reconstructed chimney incorporated numerous sandstone slabs (SS). The firebox was built to accommodate wood (W) but was eventually narrowed down to burn coal (→C). The roof over this second room was also riven board (RB), and although puncheons were originally used for the floor (P), they were eventually replaced by milled boards (→MB). The third room to the rear (iii), fashioned by Isom Slone between 1923 and 1925, was constructed not of hewn logs but of saddle-notched round ones (RL-S) of an undetermined wood type. A coal stove (CS) was installed instead of a fireplace; the room was covered by a riven board roof (RB) and had a milled-board floor (MB). None of the three rooms remains standing today (M).

The transitions illustrated in this house—hewn logs (rooms i and ii) to round logs (room iii), and wood-burning to coal-burning heat sources—will be pointedly dealt with in the succeeding chapters.

For the use of the code with outbuildings and service buildings, see the boxes below the floor plans of artifacts No. 44 and 68, respectively.

HOUSES

Figure 22. THE TANDY SLONE HOUSE (I).

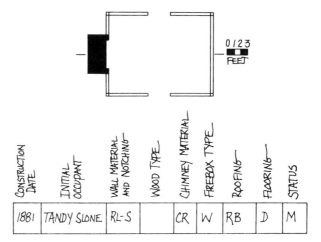

Construction Date	Initial Occupant	Wall Material and Notching	Wood Type	Chimney Material	Firebox Type	Roofing	Flooring	Status
1881	TANDY SLONE	RL-S		CR	W	RB	D	M

1. In 1881, Tandy Slone moved his family from Trace into this temporary pole house (Fig. 22) built in a wide bottom with good sun. Few pains were taken to maintain straight weathertight edges; as a result the children were wrapped in feather quilts for warmth that first winter while Tandy and Anna worked indoors.[2] After his hewn house was built (No. 2), Tandy in all probability used this structure as a barn.

Figure 23. THE TANDY SLONE HOUSE (II).

Figure 24. THE ADAM SLONE HOUSE (I).

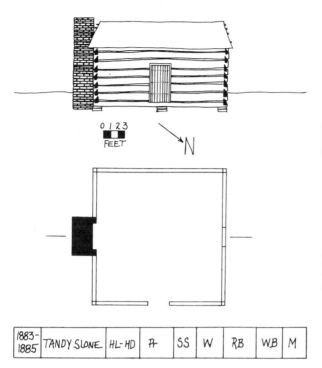

1883–1885	TANDY SLONE	HL-HD	Ħ	SS	W	RB	WB	M

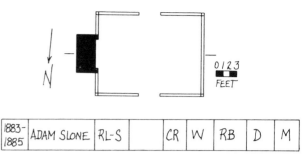

1883–1885	ADAM SLONE	RL-S		CR	W	RB	D	M

3. After following Tandy into Hollybush, Adam Slone picked a site on his father's property[5] and built this pole house (Fig. 24) in one day with the aid of Tandy and relatives from Short Fork. Within a few years, Adam and his wife, Tenia, felt prosperous enough to tear down their pole house and replace it with a hewn structure (No. 4).

2. Tandy organized another working and built this more permanent structure (Fig. 23) when he believed he had exerted the required amount of control over his immediate environment: fields had been cleared, animals pastured, and crops grown. Tandy did not remain long in Hollybush; he would live and work in a place for a limited time, soon moving on to new and inexpensive land to begin anew the same process of geographic transformation.[3]

Isaac Caudill later came into possession of the house and property, initially living in Tandy's hewn house before building his own (No. 7). Tandy's home was then designated a kitchen;[4] it later burned down or was dismantled.

Figure 25. THE ADAM SLONE HOUSE (II).

Figure 26. THE JOHN C. SLONE HOUSE.

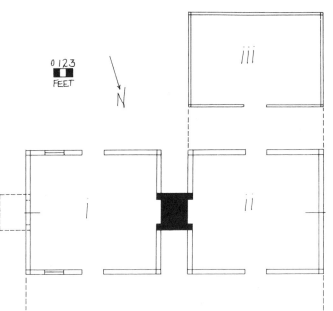

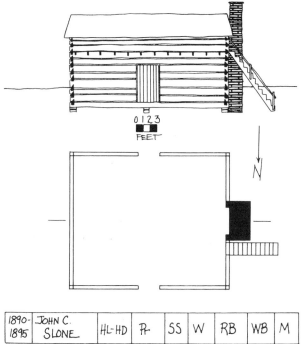

i 1887-1889	ADAM SLONE	HL-HD	P-	CR	W	RB	P	M
ii 1900-1905	ADAM SLONE	HL-HD	P-	SS	W→C	RB	P→MB	M
iii 1923-1925	ISOM SLONE	RL-S		—	CS	RB	MB	M

1890-1895	JOHN C. SLONE	HL-HD	P-	SS	W	RB	WB	M

4.   The first room of Adam's hewn house (Fig. 25i) was built on nearly the same site as his pole house.[6] When the second room was added (ii), the original chimney was torn down and reconstructed (with an additional opening) between the two rooms; Tenia's spinning wheel was stored on the porch, in the open space to the side of the chimney.

After Adam became too old to farm, he lived with one of his daughters in Trace. When he died in 1923, he was carried back over the mountain and buried in his family's graveyard (No. 64). Isom Slone, Ad's brother, then came into possession of the farm, adding the kitchen to the rear (iii).

Ad's house was dismantled in the mid-1940s, making way for yet another dwelling (No. 39).

5.   John C. Slone operated the High Rock Post Office in the upper level of this one-and-a-half-story single-pen (Fig. 26) from 1903 to 1906.[7] He drove his wagon out twice a week to pick up the mail at the post office at the mouth of Hollybush, delivering a portion of it to residents along the paths on the trip back. John C. was also known to ask people who would be traveling along his route to deliver the mail for him. His route was all through the Mallet, Nealy, and Hollybush mountains, an approximate ten-square-mile area containing about 250 people.[8] These distances were walked off·for the government with premeasured chains by John C. and young Green Slone (later to become an influential figure in the Head). In 1906 John C. gave up the job of postmaster; it passed on to Isom B. Slone, who lived at the mouth of Trace.[9]

Figure 27. THE JOHN B. SLONE HOUSE.

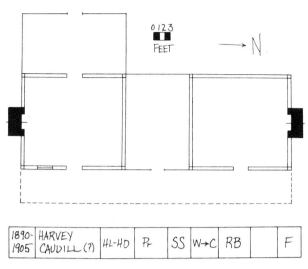

1890-1905	HARVEY CAUDILL (?)	HL-HD	Pr	SS	W→C	RB		F

Figure 28. THE ISAAC CAUDILL HOUSE.

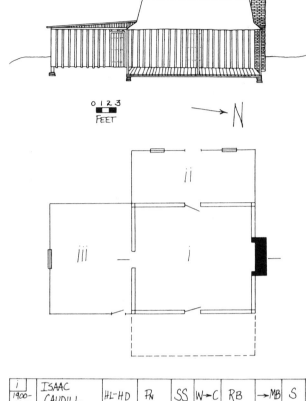

i 1900-1902	ISAAC CAUDILL	HL-HD	Pr	SS	W→C	RB	→MB	S
ii 1938	CHESTER CAUDILL	MB	—	—	CS	RB	MB	F
iii 1947	BOSS SLONE	MB	—	—	—	TP	MB	F

6. An extensive fifteen-acre bottom, ample water running past from two directions, and good sun for the crops and fruit trees were the reasons that this was the first site settled on the third branch, probably by Harvey Caudill, a relative of Isaac Caudill.[10] John B. Slone, who moved onto the farm in 1910 before passing it on to his son Mitchell in 1929, enclosed the open dogtrot (Fig. 27) with vertical boards, forming a meat room where salted pork was hung up to cure.[11]

Jasper Caudill later came into possession of the farm, transforming the house to one constructed predominantly of box (see No. 28).

7. Isaac Caudill, also known as "Stillin' Ice" for the large quantities of corn liquor he made, migrated into Hollybush from Wise Country, Virginia, and built this house (Fig. 28i) on the Tandy Slone property; he sold it to his son Franklin in 1905.[12] Chester Caudill, Franklin's son, purchased the structure in the 1930s for $50 and a heifer. Chester promptly added the rear kitchen (ii), and by the early 1940s had also covered the logs on the north and east sides with boards and battens. When he died in 1947, Boss Slone, a neighbor, built the bedroom (iii) at the request of Merdie Caudill, Chester's widow, who wanted a separate bedroom for her daughters.

Figure 29. THE HARDIN CAUDILL HOUSE.

Figure 30. THE ISOM CAUDILL/BENNER SHORT HOUSE.

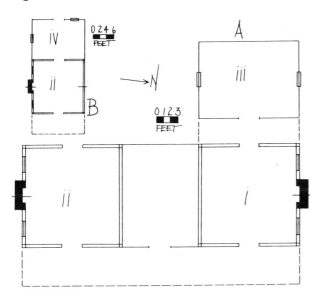

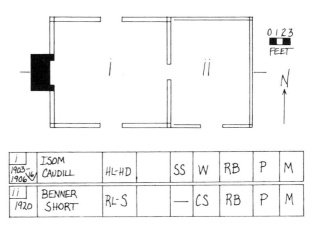

i 1903- 1906(16)	ISOM CAUDILL	HL-HD		SS	W	RB	P	M
ii 1920	BENNER SHORT	RL-S		—	CS	RB	P	M

9.   Isom Caudill, Isaac's son, died soon after the west room (i) of this house (Fig. 30) was built for him and his new wife. His widow later married Benner Short (see No. 15), also widowed, who then moved into her home and built the kitchen on the east side (ii). The Shorts left Hollybush in the 1930s.

i 1890- 1910(3)		HL-HD	P-	SS	W→C	RB	P	M
ii 1904	HARDIN CAUDILL	HL-HD	P-	SS	W→C	RB	P	F
iii 1915	HARDIN CAUDILL	MB	—	—	CS	RB	MB	M
iv 1940s		MB	—	—	CS		MB	M

8.   Hardin Caudill, the largest landowner in the Head,[14] farmed land reaching far up and down the creeks. Upon his death in the 1940s,[15] his house (Fig. 29A) passed on to relatives, who altered the structure dramatically (Fig. 29B); it later burned down.

Figure 31. THE ISOM L. SLONE HOUSE.

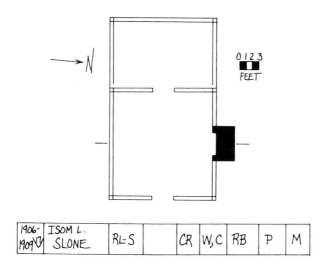

1906- 1909	ISOM L. SLONE	RL=S		CR	W,C	RB	P	M

10.   Isom L. Slone, John C.'s son, neglected to install a rear kitchen door on his house (Fig. 31), an indication of personal idiosyncrasy and not community preference. If most Head residents saw themselves as conforming to social norms, they saw Isom in the opposite light. It was customary to build a kitchen door leading to the well, but Isom, always hearing the beat of a different drummer, was content to walk out the front door and around. Since there were no windows, Isom used the fireplace and coal oil lamps for interior light. The front door was left open for illumination summer and winter, making winter visiting a sometimes cold task.

Isom eventually sold out,[18] moving into the third branch (No. 22). In the 1930s, Dowl Short (see No. 34) temporarily used the house first as a dwelling and then as a barn before dismantling it.

Figure 32. THE JOHN D. SLONE HOUSE.

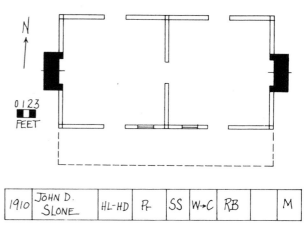

1910	JOHN D. SLONE	HL-HD	P-	SS	W→C	RB		M

11.   John D. Slone, John C.'s other son, bought property over the hill in the third branch and constructed this double-pen (Fig. 32). By the mid-1920s, however, he left the Head. His house was eventually dismantled and its components used in various buildings in the third branch.

Figure 33. THE OTHER JOHN C. SLONE HOUSE.

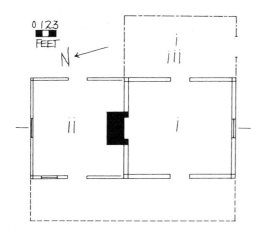

i 1910-1920	JOHN C. SLONE	HL-HD	H	SS	W→C	RB		F
ii 1940	ELLIS GIBSON	HL-HD		—		RB		M
iii 1950	CONARD SLONE	MB	—	—	CS		MB	M

Figure 34. THE DUNK CAUDILL HOUSE (I).

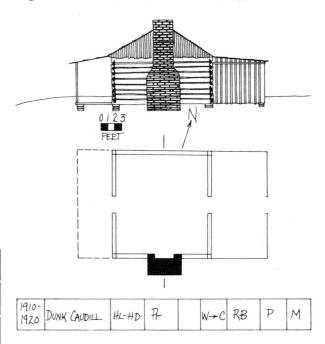

1910-1920	DUNK CAUDILL	HL-HD	H		W→C	RB	P	M

12.   Initially consisting of a log room and box kitchen (Fig. 33i), this house was built for John C. Slone (not to be confused with the postmaster) on land owned by his father John B. (No. 6).[19] In 1940 Ellis Gibson, the second owner, tore down the rear addition and built a new room (ii), buttressing it against the north wall of the original one. The third owner, Green Slone's son Conard, removed this new room in 1950, however, because of its instability, building instead a box kitchen (iii) to the rear of the first log room and thus duplicating the original floor plan.[20]

In 1960 the Slones moved out of Hollybush to an industrial area of northern Ohio, leaving the house vacant.

13.   This single-pen (Fig. 34) was the first of three houses built by John W. "Dunk" Caudill on a site noted for a large rock and a shade tree. When it was torn down in the 1930s and replaced with a round-log saddlebag (No. 27), many of its hewn logs found their way into Dunk's barn (No. 48).

Figure 35. THE BENNY CAUDILL HOUSE.

Figure 36. THE BENNER SHORT HOUSE.

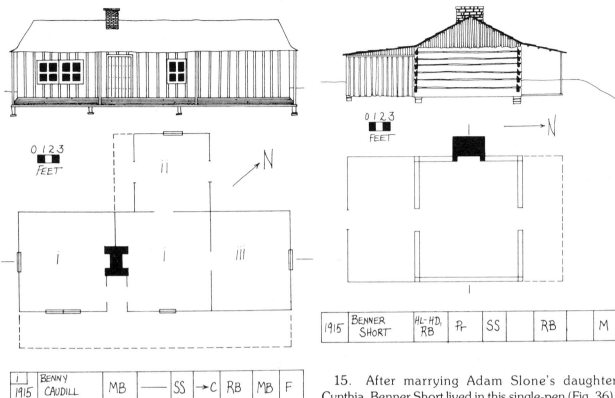

i 1915	BENNY CAUDILL	MB	———	SS	→C	RB	MB	F
ii 1915–1935	BENNY CAUDILL	MB	———	—	CS	RB	MB	M
iii 1915–1935	BENNY CAUDILL	MB	———	—	—	RB	MB	M

1915	BENNER SHORT	HL–HD, RB	Pr	SS		RB		M

14.   Dog Hall, who lived outside the Head on lower Hollybush, began operating Caney Creek's first sawmill in 1914.[21] In 1915 Benny Caudill, Hardin's son, had logs cut into boards at Dog's mill and built the first box house in the Head (Fig. 35i), shaping it like a log saddlebag. Before Benny moved out of Hollybush in 1935, he added a box kitchen to the rear (ii) and a bedroom (iii) to the north. The middle room was designated as the dining room.[22]

Marl and Verdie Huff (Hardin's daughter) were the next owners, farming the hillsides until the 1950s, when they left for Hindman so that their children could attend high school.

15.   After marrying Adam Slone's daughter Cynthia, Benner Short lived in this single-pen (Fig. 36), built by family and community members. Cynthia died soon afterward, and Benner married Isom Caudill's widow (No. 9), moving in with her.[23] Apparently, the house he shared with Cynthia either burned or was immediately dismantled, since few informants recall its existence.

Figure 37. THE TANDY SLONE HOUSE (III).

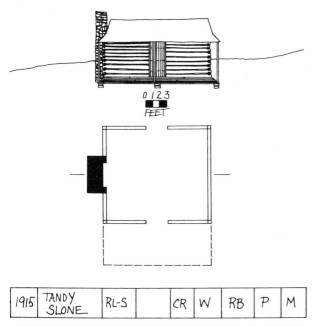

1915	TANDY SLONE	RL-S		CR	W	RB	P	M

Figure 38. THE HAWK SLONE HOUSE (I).

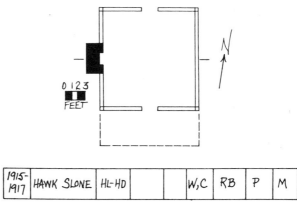

1915-1917	HAWK SLONE	HL-HD			W,C	RB	P	M

16. At Adam Slone's direction, a "retirement" house (Fig. 37) was built for his parents, Tandy and Anna, after they had become too old to work. Tandy and Anna wound up their Hollybush days in nearly the same sort of pole house in which they had begun. Their predominantly agrarian world view, however, saw that cyclical pattern as inevitable. They are said to have enjoyed living in this small house nestled to the rear of their son's farm.[24]

17. Franklin "Hawk" Slone, one of John B.'s sons, cooked in the fireplace of his single-pen (Fig. 38), built no barn, and grew no crops other than "a few roasting ears" of corn.[25] He lived by trapping, trading furs, and peddling shoelaces—made from the hides of old horses, mules, and donkeys—in area coal camps. Hawk was the local eccentric: according to legend, he hunted squirrels by knocking them out of trees with specially chosen rocks, and purposely went through life with one gallus unclipped on his overalls.[26]

This small house and its narrow site, wedged between the creek and hillside, fit Hawk's needs. Although he lived in an agricultural community, he did not take part in its rituals and thus needed little architectural or geographic space.

Figure 39. GREEN SLONE AND HIS SON AUSTIN, CIRCA 1938.

Figure 40. THE GREEN SLONE HOUSE (I).

Figure 41. THE TOM CAUDILL/WILEY CAUDILL HOUSE.

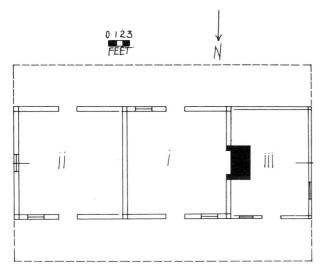

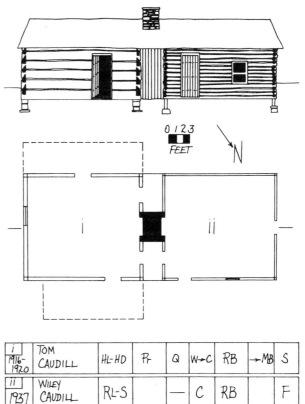

i 1916	GREEN SLONE	HL-HD	Pr	SS	W→C	RB	P	M
ii 1918	GREEN SLONE	HL-HD	Pr	—	CS	RB	P	M
iii 1920– 1925	GREEN SLONE	RL-S		—		RB		M

i 1916– 1920	TOM CAUDILL	HL-HD	Pr	Q	W→C	RB	→MB	S
ii 1937	WILEY CAUDILL	RL-S		—	C	RB		F

18.   Green Slone (Fig. 39) built the first room of his first house (Fig. 40i) prior to enlisting in the army in World War I. After being discharged eighteen months later because of an injury, he built the three-walled room to the east (ii). Green considered building a matching chimney on the east end of his new room, but instead fitted in a coal-burning stove.[27] As his family grew, Green found it necessary to add the third room (iii).

In 1935, after Green moved into his new house (No. 30), this structure was dismantled. Many of the logs were later used in his barn (No. 50) and in his son Boss's house (No. 33).

19.   Tom Caudill, soon after following his brother Dunk into the third branch, built the east room of his saddlebag (Fig. 41i). The west room (ii) was constructed by Wiley Caudill, Dunk's son, when he moved into the house in 1937.[28]

On June 30, 1940, Wiley's family was attacked by a deranged man wielding a shotgun (see Chapter 1). Wiley's nine-year-old son was killed, and his wife Ada and their newborn child were seriously injured, prompting the family to move to Ohio. Wiley did factory work for seven years before moving back into the third branch and building a new home (No. 42).[29]

Figure 42. THE JASPER CAUDILL HOUSE (I).

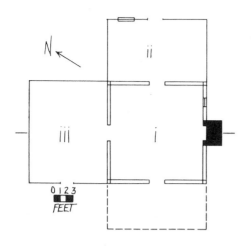

i 1920	JASPER CAUDILL	HL-HD	A	SS	W→C	RB→T		F
ii 1920-1933	JASPER CAUDILL	MB	—	—	CS	RB→T	MB	M
iii 1920-1933	JASPER CAUDILL	MB	—	—	—	RB→T	MB	M

20.   Jasper Caudill, Franklin's son, built this single-pen (Fig. 42i) near his father's house (No. 7). Before Jasper moved to the larger John B. Slone farm (No. 6) in 1934, he added the box kitchen and bedroom (ii and iii).

The board roof was replaced with tins when Vansel and Meredith Slone moved into the house in 1945. Meredith recalled their first day in the Head:

Oh, what a time of year. It was in November, and we got in there and still didn't have things set up . . . just piled up on the floor. Rain started pouring that night, and the next morning it turned to snow, and it was about twenty-eight days we never seen any sunshine. I was trying to get straightened up in the snow, and I told them I was going to move back to Caney if the sun didn't shine in Hollybush. One of my neighbor women told me, she said, "You just wait until July, and then you can see the sun."[30]

She also recalled sleeping with her children in the box bedroom while Vansel was away all week working in the coal mines in Lackey. She would wake in the morning to find the room covered with snow, which had filtered through the boards and battens.[31] The heat from the coal-burning fireplace in the log room could not sufficiently reach the box bedroom.

Vansel and his family moved out to Caney Creek in 1948 in order to cut down his traveling time to the mines.

Figure 43. THE MILES THORNSBERRY HOUSE.

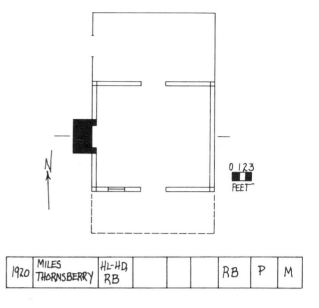

1920	MILES THORNSBERRY	HL-HD, RB			RB	P	M

21.   See Figure.43.

Figure 44. THE HENRY GIBSON/ISOM L. SLONE HOUSE.

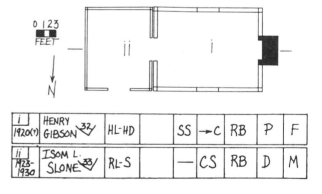

i 1920(?)	HENRY GIBSON 32/	HL-HD		SS	→C	RB	P	F
ii 1923-1930	ISOM L. SLONE 33/	RL-S		—	CS	RB	D	M

22.   See Figure 44.

Figure 45. THE HAWK SLONE HOUSE (II).

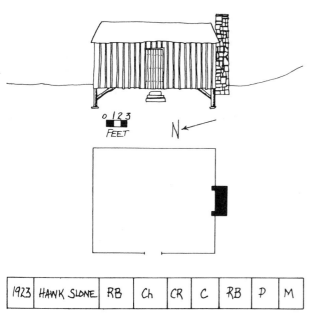

1923	HAWK SLONE	RB	Ch	CR	C	RB	P	M

23.   Hawk Slone moved out of his log house (No. 17) in about 1923, choosing to live on a "swag" a little farther up the branch. A swag is a gentle incline toward the head of a hollow or drain. Again, Hawk had neither stock, barn, nor crib. The little corn he grew was stored in his box house (Fig. 45) with him. Hawk's half-brother, Mitchell Slone (No. 6), in attempting to explain why Hawk moved from a warmer and sturdier hewn house into a leaky riven-board structure containing approximately the same amount of living space, noted that Hawk "was always taking that kind of notion."[34]

In 1930 Hawk moved over the mountain into Mallet.

Figure 46. THE JOHN HUFF HOUSE.

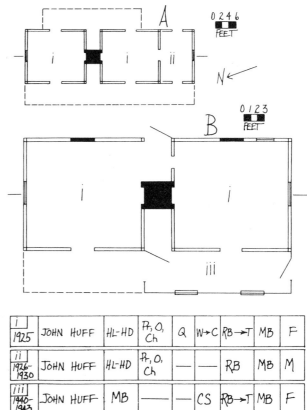

i 1925	JOHN HUFF	HL-HD	Pr, O, Ch	Q	W→C	RB→T	MB	F
ii 1926-1930	JOHN HUFF	HL-HD	Pr, O, Ch	—	—	RB	MB	M
iii 1940-1943	JOHN HUFF	MB	—	—	CS	RB→T	MB	F

24.   John Huff constructed his house (Fig. 46A) with the aid of a local builder just prior to moving his family into the Head in 1925.[35] By the early 1940s, John had sealed off the back doors and moved the rear box kitchen to the front of the house (Fig. 46B, iii). Ellis Slone, Green Slone's son-in-law, purchased the dwelling from John in 1945, tearing down a poorly built, three-sided log room on the south end (46A, ii) and covering the logs along the front of the north room with horizontal clapboards. He also replaced the original board roof with tins for style's sake. When asked if the boards had leaked, Ellis replied that although he could count the stars in the spaces between them, they kept the rain out.[36] The board floors throughout the house were later covered with linoleum.

John, for the period he owned all of the second branch, was considered one of the Head's more prominent citizens. The house, because of its multiple rooms, tin roof, and white clapboarded exterior, was thought to be one of the better homes.

Figure 47. THE GROVER CAUDILL HOUSE (I).

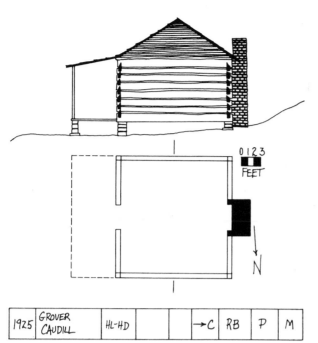

1925	GROVER CAUDILL	HL-HD			→C	RB	P	M

25.   Grover Caudill, Dunk's son, built his house (Fig. 47) with the chimney against the rear eave instead of up the gable. The chimney stones did not have to be stacked as high above the eave, a saving in time and labor. It was, however, difficult to flash a chimney against rainwater running down onto it.

Since Grover later helped build other houses with chimneys piercing the ridge (Nos. 27, 38, 40, and 42), the placement of this one was probably an experiment.

Figure 48. THE MILES JACOBS HOUSE.

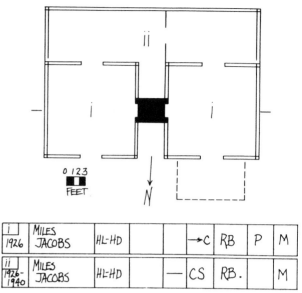

i 1926	MILES JACOBS	HL-HD			→C	RB	P	M
ii 1926-1940	MILES JACOBS	HL-HD			—	CS	RB.		M

26.   Miles Jacobs used at least one apple tree from a nearby orchard when he built his house (Fig. 48i)[37] on what had been the John D. Slone property. Miles later added a three-sided log addition to the rear of the house (ii), partitioning it into a dining room and kitchen.[38] About 1940 Miles moved out onto Caney Creek, abandoning the house.

Figure 49. THE DUNK CAUDILL HOUSE (II).

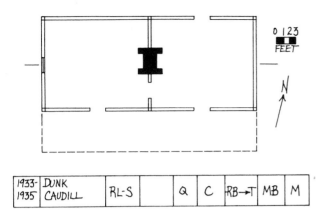

1933-1935	DUNK CAUDILL	RL-S		Q	C	RB→T	MB	M

27. Dunk, with his sons Wiley and Grover, constructed this round-log saddlebag (Fig. 49) after first dismantling his older hewn-log house (No. 13). The southwest corner of the new overhanging porch was supported by the large rock which is still used to identify the site. Dunk's grandchildren would run across the porch and slide down the rock on warm, dry days. The west room served as both a bedroom and a living room, the east as a kitchen.[39]

In the late 1940s, this house was also replaced, this time by a board-and-batten dwelling (No. 38).

Figure 50. THE JASPER CAUDILL HOUSE (II).

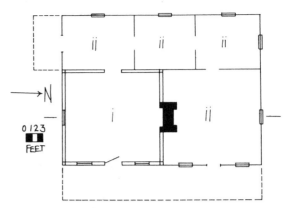

i 1890-1900	HARVEY CAUDILL (?)	HL-HD	P-	SS	W→C	RB		F
ii 1934	JASPER CAUDILL	MB	—	—	C	RB→T	MB	F

28. In 1929, John B. Slone deeded his house and property (see No. 6) to his son Mitchell, who then made his living by farming and selling excess produce at the coal camps in Wayland. Wearying of this life by 1934, Mitchell in turn sold the house and farm to Jasper Caudill (No. 20). Jasper, with the aid of his brother Chester Caudill (No. 7) and his son Oliver, promptly transformed the house from a dogtrot to a saddlebag by tearing down the south room, opening the rear of the chimney in what had been the north room (Fig. 50 i) to accommodate a coal grate, and building a box room around it (ii). At the same time he added a box addition to the rear of the house and partitioned it (from north to south) into a bedroom, dining room, and kitchen.[40]

Jasper, after about ten more years of farming and tending store (No. 71), moved out to Caney Creek and then on to Michigan.

Figure 51. THE ARTHUR SLONE HOUSE.

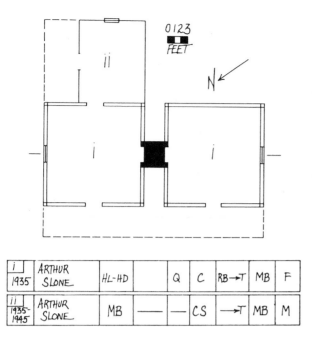

i 1935	ARTHUR SLONE	HL-HD		Q	C	RB→T	MB	F
ii 1935-1945	ARTHUR SLONE	MB	——	—	CS	→T	MB	M

29. Shortly after he married Hardin Caudill's daughter Dorothy, and wanting a home of his own, Arthur Slone asked his father Jasper, skilled at hewing and notching logs, to direct construction of this saddlebag (Fig. 51i).[41] Even though Arthur's house was located almost directly across the creek from Benny Caudill's box house (No. 14), hewn logs were used instead of the modern milled boards. Perhaps Jasper, experienced in log construction, had something to do with this decision. Later, however, Arthur did build a box kitchen to the rear (ii).

The family moved out of the Head in 1950 to take advantage of an employment opportunity.

Figure 52. THE GREEN SLONE HOUSE (II).

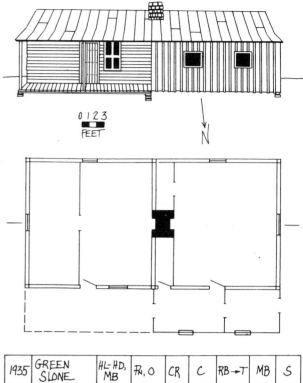

1935	GREEN SLONE	HL-HD, MB	PR, O	CR	C	RB→T	MB	S

30. Green Slone's second house (Fig. 52) was considered by his neighbors to be a large and modern structure. The front addition was divided into a kitchen and dining area; the exterior log porch wall was covered with planks to give the house a box look; and the east log room was partitioned into separate bedrooms. With the front logs hidden and the house increasing from two rooms to three and then to five, with the partitioning of the east room and kitchen, perhaps by Hollybush standards it was.

Figure 53. THE GOLDEN SLONE HOUSE (I).

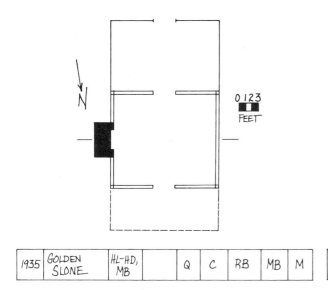

1935	GOLDEN SLONE	HL–HD, MB		Q	C	RB	MB	M

Figure 54. THE GOLDEN SLONE HOUSE (II).

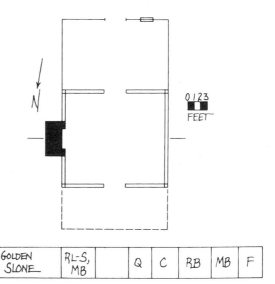

1936	GOLDEN SLONE	RL–S, MB		Q	C	RB	MB	F

31.   Since Golden Slone, John Huff's new son-in-law, had taken a job as a railroad worker in Wayland, he did not have the time to build his own house (Fig. 53). John Huff and Jake Slone constructed it for him instead, John working free and Jake being paid $40 for his labor. The site, which had been the location of the John C. Slone House (No. 5), was chosen because of a nearby spring.

Shortly after completion, the house burned in a kitchen fire. A working was immediately organized and a new house (No. 32) hastily built for Golden and his wife Laura, this time farther into the head of the second branch.[42]

32.   Golden's second house (Fig. 54) duplicated the floor plan of his first. Despite its newness, though, he and Laura soon moved out to be nearer his job. Newlyweds James and Lillie Huff moved in shortly afterward, paying John Huff, James's uncle, one-third of the corn they raised as rent. James described their moving in:

Forty-one years in December. We moved in there with a sled and a mule and took what we had into that home there. I had mighty little, you know. I drove the mule and my wife [Lillie] walked behind the sled. We had $30 to take and move in my home with. . . . I don't care for my wife telling that I lived a poor life; everybody else lived like I did back then. We had one feather bed, and we had a shuck-made straw bed [corn-shuck mattress], and bought factory [commercial fabric]— you know what factory is—and made the tick out of it . . . put them in factory, what you call a straw bed. The little post iron steads was given to me. The little iron steads didn't have the springs on it, and we went to the hills and built slats, made them out of timber, and that's the way we started.[43]

When James and Lillie moved out to Caney Creek in the early 1940s, the house passed on to another of John Huff's daughters before being abandoned.

Figure 55. THE BOSS SLONE HOUSE (I).

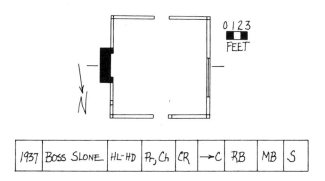

1937	Boss Slone	HL-HD	Pr, Ch	CR	→C	RB	MB	S

Figure 56. THE DOWL SHORT HOUSE.

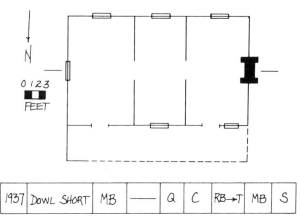

1937	Dowl Short	MB	———	Q	C	RB→T	MB	S

33.   Boss Slone borrowed many of the logs for this house (Fig. 55) from his father's first home (No. 18). Although it consisted of only one small room, Boss noted that he and his wife Zona lived here because "nobody around here was making too much money, and if we had one room that was about 15 foot square, that was all we needed. You put your bed in there, put your table in there, put your chairs and things. You had someplace to eat and that was all you needed." Zona added: "That was all we had."[44]

The newlyweds lived in this house nine years before building a larger home (No. 43) on a more level site in the second branch.

34.   Dowl Short secured the milled boards for his home (Figs. 56 and 57) by buying a box house in Trace for $25, dismantling it, and moving the lumber by corn sled over the mountain to the house site. Dowl, John Huff (his new father-in-law), and Golden Slone (temporarily laid off from his job in Wayland) then reassembled the boards, following the floor plan of the original structure. An outside opening was built into the chimney, however, to accommodate a projected future room.[45]

Dowl farmed for the eleven years he lived in the Head.[46] When he moved out of Hollybush in 1945, he sold the house to Elbert Slone, who immediately replaced the board roof with tin and partitioned the large front room into two smaller ones.[47] After six years, Elbert also moved out, deeding the house and property to Boss Slone (see Nos. 33 and 43), the last owner.

Figure 57. THE DOWL SHORT HOUSE IN 1981.

Figure 58. THE ELLIS SLONE HOUSE.

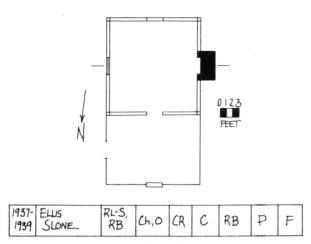

1937-1939	ELLIS SLONE	RL-S, RB	Ch,O	CR	C	RB	P	F

Figure 59. THE WILLARD CAUDILL HOUSE.

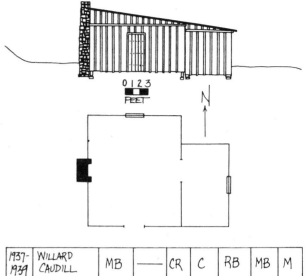

1937-1939	WILLARD CAUDILL	MB	—	CR	C	RB	MB	M

35.   A one-day working was hastily organized when it was learned that newlyweds Ellis and Tenia Slone, Green's son-in-law and daughter, wished to move into the Head. Relatives and friends came and labored from early morning until construction was completed after dark. Ellis recalled:

Well, I just had to have someplace to live. We didn't have much; we didn't use no blueprint or nothing like that. We just rented a little house (on Branham's Creek) when we first got married. And we decided to move over there on her dad's place and save the $2.00 a month rent. So I went over there and started out working, and we put out the news, and people went to coming in, and they were there with four or five mules by the next morning to haul logs.[48]

When asked what it was like to live in a house built in only one day (Fig. 58), Ellis and Tenia said that it was all they knew, and that it did have its advantages: the spaces between the puncheon floorboards, for example, meant they got plenty of fresh air. One definite drawback Ellis recalled, though, was a particular snake that would crawl through the open places between the chimney stones, stick its head into the log room, and flick its tongue at them.

A few years later, Ellis and Tenia moved into the John Huff House (No. 24). Their uninhabited house later had the reputation of being haunted.

36.   Willard Caudill's first home (Fig. 59) was built, with the assistance of his brother Chester (No. 7), of boards taken from the addition of a nearby barn. Chester was paid for his time with a new calf born to Willard's cow.[49] Willard moved in the early 1940s, when he rented the larger Adam Slone House (No. 4). He remained there only a short time, however, before taking his family out of the Head in order that his children might attend high school.

Figure 60. THE BIRCHEL SLONE HOUSE.

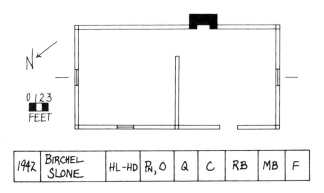

1942	BIRCHEL SLONE	HL-HD	Pᴀ, O	Q	C	RB	MB	F

Figure 61. THE DUNK CAUDILL HOUSE (III).

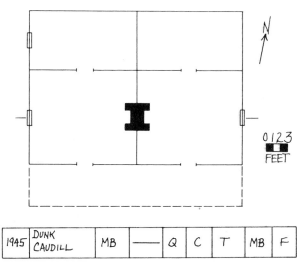

1945	DUNK CAUDILL	MB	—	Q	C	T	MB	F

37. Birchel Slone and John Huff's daughter Mony moved temporarily into Golden Slone's second house (No. 32) while constructing their own home (Fig. 60), noted for the placement of its chimney along the rear eave (nearly opposite the interior log wall). Birchel earned his living by farming and by plowing other people's gardens. He soon saw greater job opportunities outside of Hollybush and moved in the late 1940s.[50] The house passed on to one of John Huff's sons before being abandoned.

38. Dunk Caudill's third house (Fig. 61) was built on the site of the previous two (Nos. 13 and 27). Dunk and his wife Celia lived in one side of the house, and their son Grover and his wife in the other;[51] no doorways connected the two halves. Grover later built a house for himself (No. 40) and installed his parents there, selling the box house in 1949 to Martin Hall for $500. Grover reportedly needed the money to pay a hospital bill.[52]

Figure 62. THE AUSTIN SLONE HOUSE.

Figure 63. THE GROVER CAUDILL HOUSE (II).

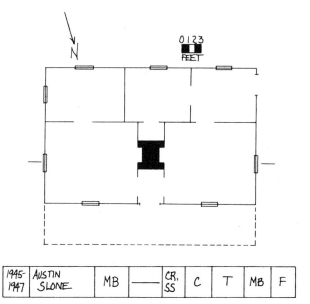

1945- 1947	AUSTIN SLONE	MB	——	CR, SS	C	T	MB	F

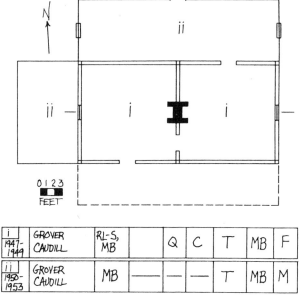

i 1947- 1949	GROVER CAUDILL	RL-S, MB		Q	C	T	MB	F
ii 1950- 1953	GROVER CAUDILL	MB	——	—	—	T	MB	M

39.   Isom Slone sold the Adam Slone House (No. 4) to Austin Slone, Adam's grandson, in the mid-1940s.[53] Austin soon dismantled Adam's hewn house, later using some of its logs to construct his barn (No. 59), and built this five-room box structure (Fig. 62). The boards, costing $25 per 1,000 board feet, were cut at Jeff Hall's sawmill on Onionblade Creek and hauled by mule and corn sled up Trace and around the ridge to a prearranged spot above the house site. Austin then skidded his lumber down the hill to the building site. Three of the house's rooms were designated as bedrooms.

Austin began working in the mines in the late 1940s. Leaving home before sunrise, he would walk over the mountain into Trace to his parked car, a distance of about a mile and a half, then drive an additional twelve miles to the mine. The trip at day's end meant that he often walked back over the mountain in the dark.[54] He and his family moved into Trace in 1960, greatly reducing his traveling time to work.

40.   See Figure 63.

Figure 64. THE CHESTER CAUDILL HOUSE.

Figure 65. THE WILEY CAUDILL HOUSE.

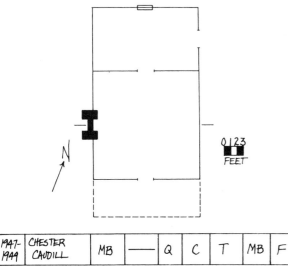

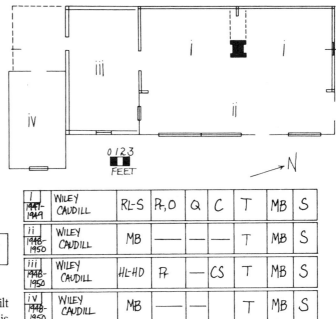

1947-1949	CHESTER CAUDILL	MB	—	Q	C	T	MB	F

i 1947-1949	WILEY CAUDILL	RL-S	Pt,O	Q	C	T	MB	S
ii 1948-1950	WILEY CAUDILL	MB	—	—	—	T	MB	S
iii 1948-1950	WILEY CAUDILL	HL-HD	Pt	—	CS	T	MB	S
iv 1948-1950	WILEY CAUDILL	MB	—	—		T	MB	S

41. Chester Caudill, Jasper's newlywed son, built this small two-room house (Fig. 64) with the aid of his brothers, Oliver and Ivan. The board exterior was covered with tar paper approximating the look of cut stones, and the chimney was constructed with a double firebox; the outside opening, however, never had its intended room built around it. On July 4, 1953, Chester and a few friends spent part of that hot day target shooting. The games over, Chester returned home and, in sliding his shotgun behind the dresser, tripped the trigger on a nail or frayed board, blowing most of his head away.[55] His widow moved out shortly afterward, and the house was never lived in again.

42. After returning to the third branch from Ohio, Wiley Caudill (see No. 19) built his family a log saddlebag (Fig. 65i) with the aid of his father Dunk and his brother Grover.[56] Within a year, Wiley had cut out the front wall, extended the width of the house six feet, and installed two large picture windows (ii). A hewn-log room (iii)[57] and a box room (iv) were later added on the south end. Commercial wallpaper was applied throughout the house, and the north and east exterior walls were covered with patterned tar paper. The log ends on the north wall were then painted with alternating blue, red, yellow, and white paint. Hedges lined the creek in front of the house, and daffodils edged the path leading up to the front door.

After its extensive revisions, the house had a spacious and slightly suburban look.

Figure 66. THE BOSS SLONE HOUSE (II).

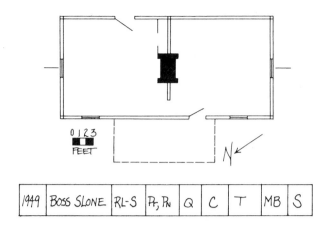

1949	BOSS SLONE	RL-S	Pt, Pn	Q	C	T	MB	S

ted the front door in the north room in an effort to create more living space in the kitchen. The back door and the large front window were intended to allow ample air circulation. In the south room, three beds were lined against the walls, leaving space to enter the house and sit around the fireplace.[58]

This was the last house built in the Head of Hollybush.

43.   Boss and Zona Slone spent $115 building their second home (Figs. 66 and 67), laying out most of the cash for roof tins. In planning the structure, Boss omit-

Figure 67. BOSS AND ZONA SLONE'S HOUSE IN 1979.

BARNS AND OUTBUILDINGS[59]

Figure 68. THE JOHN C. SLONE BARN.

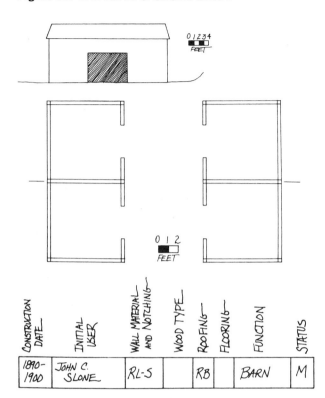

CONSTRUCTION DATE	INITIAL USER	WALL MATERIAL AND NOTCHING	WOOD TYPE	ROOFING	FLOORING	FUNCTION	STATUS
1890-1900	JOHN C. SLONE	RL-S		RB		BARN	M

44. John C. Slone's barn (Fig. 68), housing his stock, sat far in the head of the second branch, about a ten-minute walk from his home (No. 5) and in close proximity to the pasture he cleared on the western hillside. The bottoms nearer the house were initially reserved for planting. In the mid-1920s John Huff bought the entire branch, planting corn on nearly all the hillsides. His sons-in-law living in the branch with him (see Nos. 31, 32, 34, and 37) also grew corn, turning over to John as rent one-quarter of their crops. The corn John grew, as well as what he collected, was stored in the barn.

Figure 69. THE JOHN B. SLONE BARN.

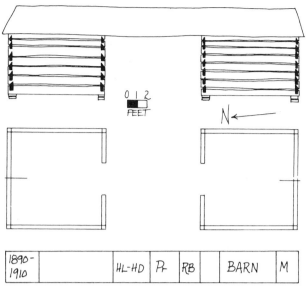

1890-1910			HL-HD	P₊	RB		BARN	M

45. See Figure 69.

Figure 70. JOHN B. SLONE'S CRIB.

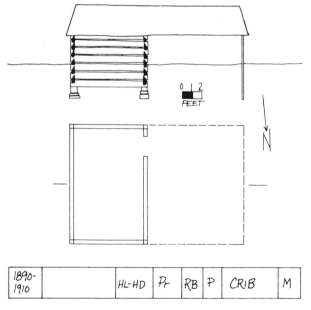

1890-1910			HL-HD	P₊	RB	P	CRIB	M

46. See Figure 70.

Figure 71. THE BENNY CAUDILL BARN.

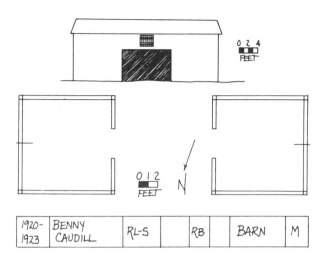

1920-1923	BENNY CAUDILL	RL-S		RB		BARN	M

Figure 72. THE DUNK CAUDILL BARN.

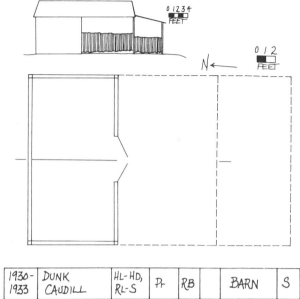

1930-1933	DUNK CAUDILL	HL-HD, RL-S	Pt	RB		BARN	S

47. As a rule, Marl Huff, the second owner of Benny Caudill's barn (Fig. 71), tossed the corn he grew through the loft window to his wife Verdie. Verdie sat on the loft floor and, as the corn flew in, quickly separated it into stock feed and corn to be mill-ground, tossing each type into its respective loft area over the stalls. The big ears were for milling, and the smaller ears for the cows, mules, and hogs (although cows would eat both large and small ears, the mules and hogs would not).

Marl eventually tore Benny's barn down because he thought it too old and because he wanted more room for his garden. It was replaced by somewhat smaller, more specialized outbuildings (No. 56, for example) to the south of the house (No. 14).[60]

48. See Figure 72.

Figure 73. ELLIS GIBSON'S HOG HOUSE.

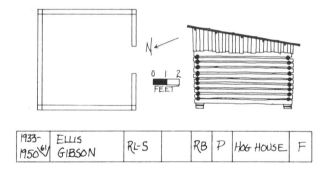

1933-1950[61]	ELLIS GIBSON	RL-S		RB	P	HOG HOUSE	F

49. Ellis Gibson's hog house (Fig. 73) had a puncheon floor, meaning that Ellis fattened his hogs "on the boards." Many Head farmers installed board floors in their hog houses; the hard surface made it uncomfortable for the cloven-hoofed animals to stand, and the hog that lay down was thought to fatten faster.

Figure 74. THE GREEN SLONE BARN.

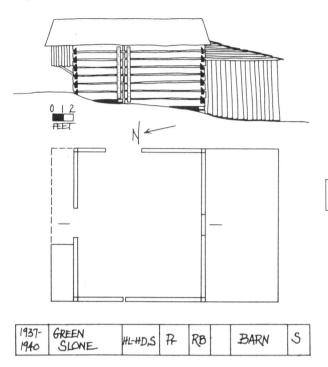

1937-1940	GREEN SLONE	HL-HD,S	Pt	RB		BARN	S

Figure 75. THE WILLARD CAUDILL BARN.

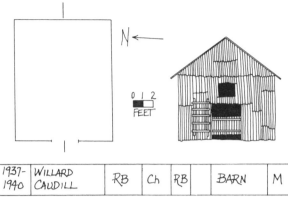

1937-1940	WILLARD CAUDILL		RB	Ch	RB		BARN		M

51. See Figure 75.

50.   Green Slone's irregularly shaped barn (Fig. 74) borrowed many of its logs from other buildings, particularly his first house (No. 18). The lower section of the barn was for stock; the loft, only three feet above ground level on the north end, was used for fodder; corn was stored in the rear addition. This outbuilding was difficult to work in and, judging by its random construction, did not seem intended for long use.

Figure 76. GOLDEN SLONE'S CRIB.

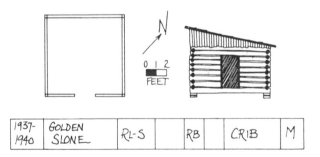

1937-1940	GOLDEN SLONE		RL-S		RB		CRIB		M

52. See Figure 76.

Figure 77. CHESTER CAUDILL'S HEN HOUSE.

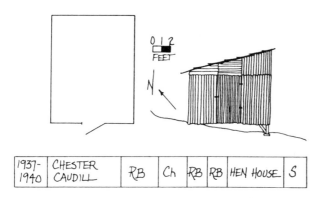

1937-1940	CHESTER CAUDILL	RB	Ch	RB	RB	HEN HOUSE	S

Figure 78. THE BOSS SLONE BARN (I).

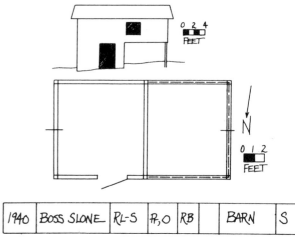

1940	BOSS SLONE	RL-S	P,O	RB		BARN	S

53. The door of Chester Caudill's hen house (Fig. 77) faced the southwest in order that anyone entering it could be seen from the house (No. 7). Chester's daughter Annabee recalled dreaming, shortly after her father died in 1947, that the hen house was being robbed. As she awoke, she realized that noises and muffled voices *were* coming from its direction, but said nothing for fear her mother would shoot at anyone outside. In the morning she told what she had heard. Her mother then went out to follow the footsteps leading from the hen house out into the snow. She located the thieves, but neither confronted them nor identified them to her children. Many years later, though, Annabee heard from another source who the culprits were and was told that while one bagged the hens, the other had a shotgun trained on the front door of the house, ready to shoot whoever might open it.[62]

54. The overhang of Boss Slone's barn (Fig. 78) was used to keep tackle, tools, and other equipment dry.[63] Charlie Hall, the schoolteacher, also tied his horse underneath after riding into the Head and before walking down the steep hill to the schoolhouse. The stall housed Boss's mule, and the loft stored the fodder.

Figure 79. MARL HUFF'S SMOKEHOUSE.

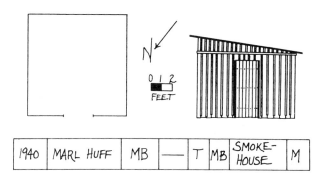

1940	MARL HUFF	MB	——	T	MB	SMOKE-HOUSE	M

Figure 80. THE MARL HUFF BARN.

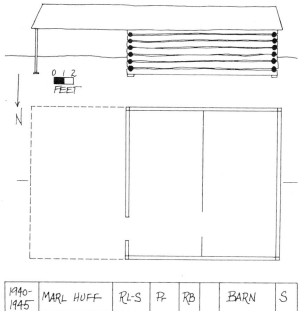

1940-1945	MARL HUFF	RL-S	P̶	RB	BARN	S

55. Marl's smokehouse (Fig. 79) was intended to protect his sometimes 1,000 pounds of preserved meat from rodents, insects, itchy fingers, and the elements. Cats were his most serious problem, though, making it necessary to nail the wall boards securely to the sills.

Marl smoked his meat by putting hickory chips in a metal pan or bucket and maintaining a smoldering fire for three days. He used no flue, instead allowing the smoke to escape through the cracks between the boards.[64] In the Head, however, meat was customarily salted rather than smoked by being cooled for two weeks, hand-packed with salt, and then allowed to cure in the smokehouse for three more weeks. By then the meat was ready to be cooked and eaten. Regardless of process used, such a structure was always referred to as the "smokehouse."

After moving out of Hollybush in 1958, Marl later returned to disassemble his smokehouse. He rebuilt it at his new home in Hindman, but this time used it to house chickens.

56.   See Figure 80.

Figure 81. THE BIRCHEL SLONE BARN.

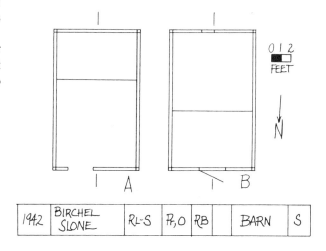

1942	BIRCHEL SLONE	RL-S	P̶,O	RB	BARN	S

57.   See Figure 81.

Figure 82. ELLIS SLONE'S CRIB.

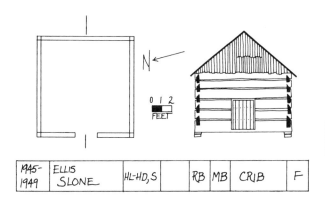

1945–1949	ELLIS SLONE	HL-HD, S		RB	MB	CRIB		F

58. See Figure 82.

Figure 83. THE AUSTIN SLONE BARN.

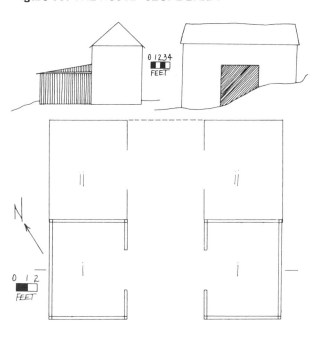

i 1947–1949	AUSTIN SLONE	HL-HD, RL-S	Pt, O	RB		BARN	S
ii 1947–1949	AUSTIN SLONE	RB		RB		BARN	F

59. Many of the logs in Austin Slone's barn (Fig. 83) were borrowed from other structures, particularly Adam Slone's second house (No. 4).[65] The logs, from bottom to top, ran from hewn to round and from half-dovetailed to saddle-notched. The rear addition was box construction.

Figure 84. WILEY CAUDILL'S CRIB.

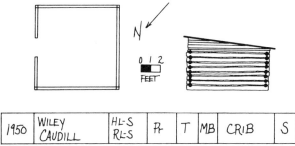

1950	WILEY CAUDILL	HL-S RL-S	Pt	T	MB	CRIB	S

60. See Figure 84.

Figure 85. THE BOSS SLONE BARN (II).

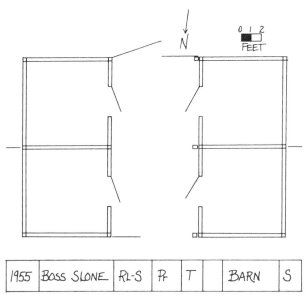

1955	BOSS SLONE	RL-S	Pt	T	BARN	S

61. Five years after moving into Dowl Short's house (No. 34), Boss Slone constructed this barn (Fig. 85) during a period of unemployment. Since Boss could not find trees long enough for the barn's 27-foot loft, the east and west cribs were built independently of each other. By buttressing the unconnected parts under one roof, he gave the outbuilding its intended unified appearance.[66]

COAL BANKS

62. This multiple-faced coal bank (Fig. 86) was first opened about 1915 on land belonging to Franklin Caudill (see No. 7). Many residents on the first and second branches, who had little or no access to coal on their own property, came down the path and mined coal here for their heating and cooking needs. The owners of this exposed seam were considered "good neighbors" in that they were willing to share their resources.

The mining process consisted of first digging straight back into the 40-inch-high vein with mattocks, and then bracing the layer of slate above with log piers in order to prevent it from collapsing. When a tunnel, or "room," had been dug, blasting powder rolled in newspaper or magazine pages was inserted in holes augered low in the vein, tamped with a long stick, and ignited. The coal blew forward, ever lengthening the tunnel. The loosened coal was then shoveled into small wagons and hauled out of the mine by hand. In the 1930s, round pipe was laid on the tunnel floor so that the wagons, set on lipped factory wheels, could be rolled out more easily. Each user was expected to shore up newly mined areas with timbers, leaving them safe for the next person.[67]

Since it could take up to four days to mine the 200 bushels of coal necessary to heat a house for a winter, families incapable of mining their own fuel hired neighbors, paying them through work exchange. One form of repayment was for parents to send their children to hoe the neighbors' cornfields on a day-for-day basis. In this way, cash—always in short supply—did not have to change hands.[68]

63. Tom Caudill (see No. 19) owned a coal bank, also opened about 1915, which served the energy needs of third-branch residents. Here, though, only small hand-pulled wagons were used. Once out of the mine, the coal was loaded into sleds that held about eight bushels each and resembled miniature corn sleds, even retaining the name "corn sleds" when coal was the cargo. The sled sides were constructed of strong and pliable white oak, while hickory or locust was used for the runners because of their resistance to splitting under heavy weights.[69]

Figure 86. THE SUPPORTED INTERIOR OF FRANKLIN CAUDILL'S COAL BANK.

GRAVEYARDS

Funeral practices in Hollybush remained relatively constant through 1960. No outside agency was called in to tend to the deceased. Rather, the straight-walled casket was made in the Head of local woods; the wake took place in the main room of the departed's house; and the body was carried to the family graveyard and buried by relatives, neighbors, and friends.

64.   Ad Slone's family graveyard lies on a hillside opposite the site of his house (No. 4). The majority of the sandstone markers have hand-chiseled inscriptions, giving names and sometimes dates. Ad and Tenia's graves are covered with a gravehouse, a once popular structure in the region (Fig. 87) but rare today. Built ostensibly to keep weather off the graves, its other use was to prevent "graverobbers," small and mysterious animals believed to dig down through the freshly turned dirt, from feeding off the deceased.[70]

Because of both the high rate of illiteracy in this region at the turn of the century[71] and the lack of a stone-carving tradition, a carefully constructed gravehouse may have fulfilled the same need to do well by the deceased, materially and visually, that is demonstrated by the meticulously inscribed tombstones of other regions.

65.   The Caudill family graveyard, on the hillside behind the Isaac Caudill house (No. 7), is marked only by tall reed grasses and two unmarked headstones,
both chipped to an angular top. Yet many people are buried here; their graves were once designated with wooden crosses which have rotted and fallen away. Chester Caudill and an infant son are known to be interred here, as is Chester's daughter Ethel. Ethel died in Ohio in 1977, and her body was brought back to the Head in a four-wheel-drive vehicle through the January snows. Axes were used to chop through the frozen ground so that her wish to be buried at home, next to her father, could be fulfilled.[72]

66.   Green Slone chose a site farther downstream for his family's graveyard, possibly because the extended family's cemetery (No. 64) was full. There are only four graves; three have head and foot stones made of molded cement, which were hand-inscribed while still wet. Green's headstone, the exception, is one of those supplied by the U. S. Army to deceased World War I veterans. Nearly all tombstones in the Head were commercially produced after Green died in 1953.

67.   In the mid-1930s a stretch of flat hillside along the third branch was also designated a graveyard. Enclosed within a wire fence are six identifiable graves: John W. "Dunk" Caudill, 1880–1972; Celia Caudill, 1870–1958; Chester Caudill, 1932–1953; Ivan Caudill, 1926–1954; Roscoe Nolan, 1901–1969; and John Nolan, 1959–1960. A few stones are of hand-inscribed concrete. Most, though, are factory-inscribed marble, standard in shape and cleanly lettered.

Figure 87. GRAVEHOUSES, circa 1900 (Alice Lloyd College Photographic Archives).

SERVICE BUILDINGS

Figure 88. THE SCHOOLHOUSE.

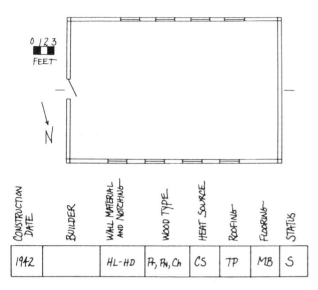

CONSTRUCTION DATE	BUILDER	WALL MATERIAL AND NOTCHING	WOOD TYPE	HEAT SOURCE	ROOFING	FLOORING	STATUS
1942		HL-HD	Pt, Pn, Ch	CS	TP	MB	S

68.   It had become habit for children in the Head to walk two and a half miles one way in order to attend the school at Middle Hollybush, the closest available. Parents had tried numerous times to have a school located nearer; in the early 1940s the county school board finally consented to supply a teacher if the community would build a schoolhouse.[73] The community agreed to this condition, heartily gathering for this one last working. Hobart Watson, who lived in the Head of Trace, lent his mules to snake the logs off the hilltops and down to a site donated by Green Slone. Older men with hewn-log experience, like Green himself and John Huff, directed the eight- to nine-day project (Figs. 88 and 89), to which many contributed their labors.[74]

Nan Taylor, a former student, recalled how the school operated in the early 1950s:

Let's see, school started in about September. We'd go until the last of May or the first of June before we'd get out. [Prior to the 1950s the school ran from September to March so the children could be free for the planting season.] So through those spring months I would miss a lot, plus sometimes through the winter months, but I never missed because of the weather. I missed because Mom would need me at home.

Charlie [Hall, the teacher at the school for nearly ten years] lived at the mouth of Trace, and walked or rode a mule, and he really had a hard time, Charlie did. It was amazing, you know, they didn't get paid very much back then, and it's amazing that he would have even gone over there.

Our lunches—we had a table setting right back in there and we had our little lard bucket, you know, one of those little four-pound buckets [to carry the lunch meal in], and we'd just each one set our lunches on the table, and we would take milk and bread for lunch. And I remember when we would go in the springtime, Mom would cook green beans and cornbread and an onion head. I can remember that was a good meal. . . .

There was just one big stove right in the middle, and we

would freeze in the wintertime. You'd get so cold that you'd have to set with your coat on. It'd be so cold. The back of [the school] used to be cleared more than now, and we'd play tag; we could just play there all day if Charlie would let us.[75]

By the late 1950s the county school board, increasingly mindful of consolidation, refused to further finance a teacher's salary, forcing the school to close (Fig. 90). In 1978 Ellis Slone (No. 35), one of its builders, bought the building at a land auction because he, as he said, was "fond of the old school."

Figure 89. THE SCHOOLHOUSE IN 1979.

Figure 90. HOLLYBUSH SCHOOLCHILDREN: one of the last classes to attend the school. Frances Owens, the teacher, appears on the far right; some mothers and grandmothers stand in the back row (courtesy Irene Slone).

Figure 91. GREEN SLONE'S GRISTMILL.

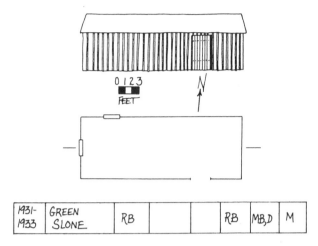

1931-1933	GREEN SLONE	RB			RB	MB,D	M

Figure 92. GREEN SLONE'S BLACKSMITH SHOP.

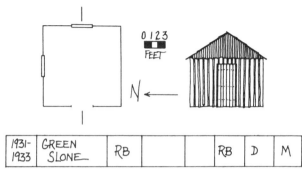

1931-1933	GREEN SLONE	RB			RB	D	M

69.   Green Slone's gristmill (Fig. 91) was located a short distance down the path from his second house (No. 30). The mill was powered by an eight-horse-power gasoline engine,[76] which was connected to the hopper by an 18-foot-long canvas belt, determining in large part the building's shape. The door and windows were placed to best illuminate these two principal components.

Green's customers, from the first and second branches as well as over the mountain in Mallet, shelled their corn before coming to the mill (the cobs were saved and used as stove fuel). Green then ground the kernels into the heavy meal used to make corn bread, corn muffins, and corn sticks; to bread fried chicken; and to mix with bacon grease for cornmeal gravy. In order to defray costs, Green collected a percentage of the corn he had ground, about one-seventh of each bushel, in a container called the "toll bucket."[77]

70.   Green Slone collected scrap iron for his blacksmith shop (Fig. 92) from wherever possible and used it to forge such farm accessories as hinges, horse and mule shoes, and hoe blades. The latter, called "laid hoes," were fashioned from rectangular pieces of old crosscut saws. If a hoe was to be used by a man on a corn-covered hillside, Green made the blade approximately 10 inches wide and 6 inches high. A woman's hoe for the same place and purpose was only 6 inches wide, and thus lighter and easier for her to use. Garden hoes were made 2 inches shallower in order to protect vegetable root systems, and their sharp corners filed to a blunt curve so as not to damage plants in adjoining rows. Green fitted all hoe blades with a walnut or hickory handle, worked round and smooth with a pocketknife.[78]

When Green died in 1953, his shop ceased operation.

Figure 93. JASPER CAUDILL'S STORE.

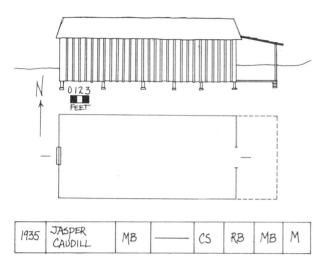

1935	JASPER CAUDILL	MB	———	CS	RB	MB	M

71.   Once a week Jasper Caudill, whose store (Fig. 93) supplied goods to third-branch residents, drove his wagon out to Caney or sometimes all the way to Wayland to pick up supplies. Since electricity was not available in the Head until the late 1940s, only foods not requiring refrigeration—rice, sugar, oatmeal, cocoa, coffee, and pinto beans, for example—could be stocked. Jasper also sold such hardware as metal water dippers, buckets, dishpans, horseshoes, and roofing nails, and a limited number of clothing items—gloves, socks, and women's hose.

Figure 94. JASPER CAUDILL'S BLACKSMITH SHOP.

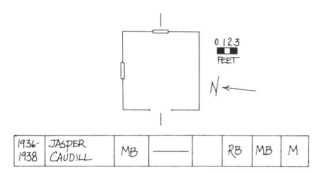

1936- 1938	JASPER CAUDILL	MB	———		RB	MB	M

72.   Jasper, like Green Slone, used a push-bellowed forge in his blacksmith shop (Fig. 94), fashioning chains and horseshoes from scrap iron collected at the local mines. He also fired and hammered out new points for plows that had been dulled in the Head's rocky soil.

Figure 95. JASPER CAUDILL'S GRISTMILL.

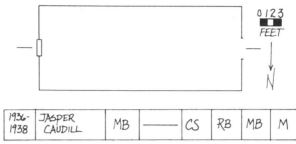

1936- 1938	JASPER CAUDILL	MB	———	CS	RB	MB	M

73.   Jasper's hopper sat near the doorway of his gristmill (Fig. 95) for light and for ease in handling orders; the engine[79] was located at the opposite end, near the window.

On Friday mornings, Jasper's customers dropped off their corn in emptied bean, coffee, and sugar sacks, each identified by a colored swatch sewn in one of the upper corners. Throughout the day he milled the corn, resacking it in the original containers, which he lined up inside the doorway. Jasper's customers returned in the late afternoon or evening, often after he had left, to collect their sacks. His fee was one quart per bushel of the unmilled kernels. If during the week a neighbor ran out of meal, Jasper would grind corn on request, not deferring the task until the following Friday.

Beginning in the 1930s, Jasper's sons began to migrate out of the Head toward Michigan and factory work. By the mid-1940s, they finally lured him into following them with tales of high wages for work that was hard but still easier than hoeing corn on the hillside. Jasper finally relented, moving first to Caney and then on to Michigan at age 47,[80] and his third-branch customers began to take their grocery, milling, and blacksmithing needs over the mountain to Green Slone.

Figure 96. GREEN SLONE'S STORE.

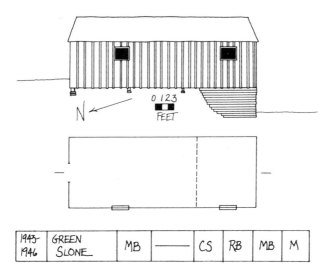

1943–1946	GREEN SLONE	MB	—	CS	RB	MB	M

74.   Green began operating his store (Fig. 96) shortly after Jasper Caudill left Hollybush. He transported his stock once a week by corn sled from the mouth of Trace, where the grocery supplier dropped off his order at Charlie Hall's store. When the creek waters were high, Green stretched canvas across the bottom of the sled to keep moisture away from his goods. Three items stocked were flour, sugar, and small crackers packed in barrels. Green, not being able to read, write, or do sophisticated arithmetic, devised his own pricing method: he put slash marks, each representing a nickel, on his stock with a crayon and counted the slashes; when he reached twenty, he laid a nail on the counter, denoting a dollar. A nail and three slashes, for example, meant goods totaling $1.15.[81] Since the community still supplied much of its own food, Green's inventory was naturally limited. Eventually, though, he began carrying salted bacon and cans of evaporated milk; by 1950 many residents had stopped preserving meat and keeping cows.

Green's store closed soon after his death in 1953. Consumer items, which had become increasingly relied upon, were then obtainable only on the outside. The demarcation between the old self-sufficient ways and the new was now sharply drawn and the trend irreversible.

4. Changes

Although the lifespan of the Head of Hollybush community was relatively short, only about eighty years, many architectural changes occurred, gathering concerted momentum in the 1930s as the social structure of the community was altered.

The first of these architectural changes, paralleling a changing attitude of a people towards its shelter, was the exclusion of the sleeping lofts that were traditional elsewhere. Only one house in the Head, John C. Slone's (No. 5), included a loft, even though sleeping lofts were being regularly built in close proximity to the Head up to the 1930s, many right over the hill in Trace. Builders like Isaac Caudill (No. 7), Tandy Slone (No. 2), and Harvey Caudill (No. 6) were uncomfortable enough with their decision to omit the loft that they built their houses one and a half stories high, even though they had no upper floor, only a light ceiling to accommodate minor storage. Possibly extra height meant that a sleeping loft could have been added later if the need or inclination arose.

It would have been relatively simple, though, to install the upper floor as the logs were being stacked, so it seems that the extra height was intended to give the appearance of traditionality while hiding the internal changes. Green Slone went so far as to notch ceiling joists into the front and rear walls of his first house (No. 18),[1] yet he did not use this potential upper story to spread out his family's living space. Rather, when space was needed, another room was laboriously added.

Among informants, consensual explanation for the omission of the loft was that the builders simply chose not to include it in the design. Since design elements in folk building along Upper Caney can change from one side of a mountain to the other, this suggests that small pockets of architectural subtraditions may exist, based on extended family or community preference.

Between approximately 1900 and 1915, the plate— or wall log—began habitually to be set 9 feet above ground level instead of 12,[2] demonstrating that builders had grown comfortable enough with their one-story houses to further alter the design and leave out the four or five logs previously stacked above the ceiling poles.

Concurrent with the move toward one-story buildings was a decrease in room size. The three hewn-log houses built between approximately 1883 and 1890 were all at least 18 by 20 feet.[3] After 1890 the tendency was to build somewhat smaller rooms. Isaac Caudill, John B. Slone (No. 6), and Isom Caudill (No. 9), all lived in houses with 16-by-18-foot rooms, built between 1890 and 1906. House sizes decreased even more beginning about 1915 and stayed fairly constant after that, mostly with rooms about 14 by 16 feet.[4]

Yellow poplar logs were initially used in construction,[5] but as time progressed, other woods such as oak and chestnut were chosen. One obvious explanation for the change in wood types was that poplar was sold early on to the timber merchants. Given the choice between cash and easily workable wood, most Head builders found themselves willing to substitute the other woods, even though the trees might be smaller and the lumber harder to work. The necessary mental adjustments were made to tolerate these qualities. For example, when Boss Slone built his first house (No. 33) in 1935, using poplar logs taken from his father's first house, chestnut was used to finish the structure when the borrowed logs ran out.[6]

The way hewn logs were shaped was also modified. The early logs had all the bark removed by hewing the tops and bottoms as well as the sides.[7] By around 1900 the barked tops and bottoms were no longer hewn.[8] Builders possibly thought that mud chinking would hold better in a curved and rough-textured surface, but more important, omitting this step saved time. Eventually, the hewing of logs waned and builders began favoring first round-log and then box houses. An example of the move from hewn to round can be seen in the Tom Caudill / Wiley Caudill house (No. 19): the hewn-log room was built by Tom in about 1918, and the round-log one about 1937 by Wiley. Wiley could have duplicated the hewn style of nearby houses like Adam Slone's (No. 4) and Hardin Caudill's (No. 8), but he chose to build with small saddle-notched logs, approximating the size and shape of the existing room with far less time and work. The first house built by Dunk Caudill (No. 13) was hewn, but the second one, built in the 1930s (No. 27), was round. After Golden Slone was burned out of his hewn-log house (No. 31), a round-log structure (No. 32) was built instead for him and his family. Boss Slone first built a hewn-log house (No. 33) and later one of round logs (No. 43). His father, Green Slone, added a round-log room to his original hewn house (No. 18).[9]

The box house seems the next logical evolutionary move after the shift from hewn logs to round ones; it would be comforting to think of the eclipse of the older building traditions as rigidly following clearly defined steps: hewn to round to box. And in some instances they did: Dowl Short (No. 34), Boss Slone, and Dunk Caudill all moved from round-log to box houses. In most cases, though, people built box houses after having lived in hewn ones,[10] leaping over what might be considered the middle step, the round-log house. It can be argued, though, that builders who went directly from hewn logs to box construction were aware of the round-log alternative built by others[11] and did not feel the need to duplicate that step themselves.

At any rate, the gradual demise of hewn-log building is clear: of the twenty-nine houses built in 1935 and before, excluding early pole houses, twenty-three were hewn; of the eleven houses built afterward—excluding Boss Slone's (No. 33), which borrowed its shaped logs—only two were hewn. Clearly, something occurred to cause builders to change to a new material (milled boards) or to treat the old ones differently. One explanation, that the large trees required for hewing

had been cleared or sold off by 1935, would not be valid: the logs in the schoolhouse (No. 68), built in 1942, were over 30 feet long and 1 to 1½ feet high after shaping, and they were cut from trees growing along the ridges between the first and second branches. Proper-sized trees were available, but to pursue that type of architectural technology was no longer of the people's choosing.

The shift away from hewn logs was also visible in barns and other outbuildings. John B. Slone's crib (No. 46) was constructed of hewn logs before 1910, but when Ellis Gibson's hog house (No. 49) was built only four feet away, sometime between 1933 and 1950, the logs were left round. John B.'s crib could also be compared to Golden Slone's crib (No. 52), built of round logs about twenty-five years later in the 1930s. Both were set high off the ground, yet enough time had passed that Golden no longer wanted to duplicate the older log treatment. Since barns disappeared from the Head of Hollybush more quickly than houses, the hewn sample is relatively small, yet all older informants (in their seventies, eighties, and nineties) recall that the vast majority of older outbuildings were built of hewn logs. There were exceptions of course: John C. Slone's barn (No. 44) was built around 1900, and its logs were round. What is worth noting here, however, is that many hewn-log barns were built prior to 1925 and very few later. Of the twenty-five known barns and cribs built after 1925, excluding those that borrowed hewn logs from other buildings,[12] twenty-two were either round-log or box construction. The shift can also be clearly seen in smokehouse construction. Older informants recalled all the older smokehouses being built of hewn logs. Those constructed after 1935 were all box, as were the stores, gristmills, and blacksmith shops.

The workmanship of many of the outbuildings also deteriorated through time: when John B. Slone's barn and crib (Nos. 45 and 46) are compared with the barns of Green Slone and Marl Huff (Nos. 50 and 56), built years later, it becomes apparent that the latter builders did not want to invest as much time and energy in outbuilding construction as did the earlier ones. The bark-covered round logs in Boss Slone's barn (No. 54) are fast decaying. The hewn logs in surviving cribs thirty to forty years older have only lately begun to decompose. Wiley Caudill's crib (No. 60), built about 1960, is set low to the ground and covered with a watertight tin roof, yet it is collapsing because of its poorly notched logs.

As workmanship declined, sometimes so did size. The difference between the older 10-foot-square barn stalls and the newer 9-foot ones is negligible, but when the older two- and four-stall barns are compared with those built after 1935, the change becomes more apparent. Barns the size of Birchel Slone's (No. 57—10 by 14 feet, including two stalls and a loft) or Marl Huff's (containing two stalls and a loft, all in an 8-foot-high structure) seem to suggest that some of the later builders no longer wanted or needed large barns and scaled their buildings down accordingly. In years previous, dietary needs dictated outbuildings of a relatively consistent size from farm to farm. Families could not have gotten by with a barn the size of Birchel's or Marl's to shelter their animals and much of their harvested food supply; they needed larger structures like those of John C. (No. 44) or John B. Slone.

Slats split from oak or chestnut were originally used as fencing, chinking between logs, and gable enclosures; eventually they were used to construct whole rooms. The same technology was later applied to milled-board structures. By the mid-1930s vertical boards, although not new to the region, were beginning to be considered in the Head as an alternative to log construction. When Chester Caudill built his hen house (No. 53) and his brother Willard built his barn (No. 51), both in the 1930s, they saved time and labor by using riven boards. In the 1940s Austin Slone used them to double the floor space of his double-crib barn (No. 59). By the time milled boards were commonly available, the way had already been prepared for their acceptance. If splitting boards was easier than cutting, snaking, and notching logs, then buying the boards ready cut was an even bigger bonus. But what of the cost? To many, it must have been prohibitive, but other builders evidently thought the expense preferable to the time and labor required by the older system, because they paid the price.[13] Some paid not only to construct new buildings and additions but even to cover existing structures. Upon remodeling his house in the 1930s, Jasper Caudill (No. 28) covered the south log room with boards and battens so that the rooms, although originally made of contrasting materials, would match.[14] Chester Caudill was instructed by his wife Merdie, about the same time, to cover the front of their hewn-log house (No. 7), one of the most technically ideal in the Head, with box.[15] Green Slone and Ellis Slone both, between 1940 and 1946, bought and applied horizontal boards to the fronts of their hewn-log houses.[16]

Another material change occurring after 1935 was the adaptation of the tin or aluminum roof, regarded as an improvement over riven boards. Tins were introduced into the Head by Green, Ellis, and Elbert Slone, who pooled their resources for an order large enough to re-cover their roofs in 1945.[17] Ellis noted that they did not actually keep the rain out better than boards, but they certainly looked tighter. They were also attractive

when new, pleasant-sounding on rainy days, and expensive. An 8-by-2-foot section of the grooved type most commonly used in the county cost $2.00.[18] Projecting that unit figure for a 14-by-32-foot saddlebag, an overhanging roof with a 6 / 12 pitch would have cost about $70; a 12 / 12, about $90. Right after World War II, $90 was considered by informants to be a great deal of money, especially when one could buy, for example, a three-room house, three outbuildings, and twenty acres of cleared land—including a coal bank—for $600.[19] In 1949 Boss Slone spent $115 to build his round-log house, and as previously noted, acknowledged that most of the money went into the tins. The older-style board roof could be split by hand at little or no cost; however, doing so required time and know-how. For most builders tins became the accepted choice,[20] implying one or any combination of four contingencies: (1) the structural benefits of tin far outweighed those of board, no matter how excessive the cost; (2) it was preferable to buy tins rather than to take the time and energy to split and install boards; (3) the cost of hiring someone to split boards was close enough to the cost of tin to swing builders into the metal's camp; (4) the skills needed to split boards were being either fast abandoned or forgotten. The first contingency does

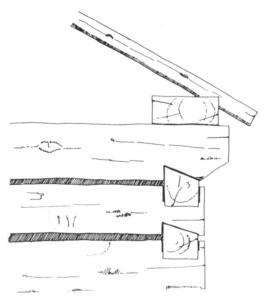

Figure 97. PLATE ASSEMBLY IN THE ISAAC CAUDILL HOUSE is representative of the older style.

not correspond well with informants' sentiments, but a combination of the second, third, and fourth does, suggesting that the older concepts of how time and energy should be spent and what traditional skills should continue to be reinforced were undergoing revision. It was becoming preferable to embrace what was new and what freed the builder for other tasks.

As house coverings changed, so did some of the internal structural techniques used to support them. Plates, as previously mentioned, once overhung the wall (Fig. 97), but as time passed, many receded: when Green Slone's house (No. 30) was built in 1935, for example, the plate had only a 3-inch overlap (Fig. 98). The overhanging plate had a short renaissance in the schoolhouse in 1942, but by the mid-1940s plates were

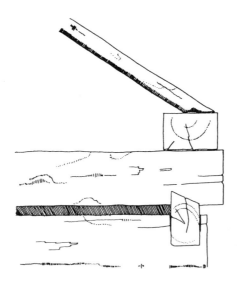

Figure 98. PLATE ASSEMBLY IN THE GREEN SLONE HOUSE (II), built in 1935, represents the newer style.

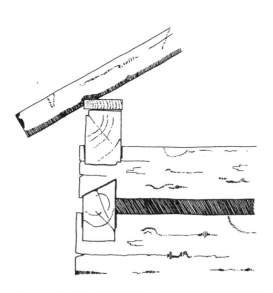

Figure 99. PLATE ASSEMBLY IN THE WILEY CAUDILL HOUSE, built in the late 1940s.

being set flush with the wall (Fig. 99). Although informants were not able to articulate a cause, a small amount of time and energy would have been saved by not cutting the top gable-end logs longer to support an overhanging plate, and by not having to roll or hoist the plate over the lips of the top end logs. The manner in which many of the rafters met the plate also changed. In the older style, the rafters overhung, resting in notches cut into the plate. In most houses assembled between 1925 and 1937,[21] however, the rafter ends were cut on an angle and nailed flush to the plate top (see Fig. 98).

The manner in which rafters were fastened at the ridge remained relatively constant. Most were cut to fit flush at the ridge and were pegged or nailed together

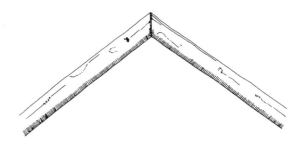

Figure 100. THE PREFERRED FORM OF RAFTER ASSEMBLY.

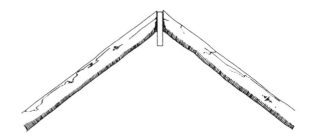

Figure 101. RIDGEBOARD AND RAFTER ASSEMBLY.

(Fig. 100).[22] Rafter material changed somewhat; milled boards replaced the traditional round poles,[23] pushing the construction cost up slightly but saving time and labor. Only two houses,[24] both built late, used ridgeboards (Fig. 101). Once a ridgeboard had been stretched from gable apex to gable apex, a builder could fasten the rafters himself. A pattern of adopting new materials and techniques, partly to free the once obligatory help, was becoming a predominant practice through the 1930s and 1940s.

The early hewn-log houses had a scarcity of wall openings; one informant recalled their having only one permanently fixed window or wooden shutter.[25] Many smaller houses built later had no window openings at all and were lit by the fireplace, lamps, and open doors. James Huff recalled how he lit his windowless home (No. 32): "We used an oil light, an oil lamp. When we didn't have that, we used grease lights. Took can [jar] lids and put grease in them and got a cotton rag and put it down here and got it wet, and then put the other lid over it and burnt it."[26] The lid on top controlled the amount of oxygen and helped prevent flare-ups.

Even though a small number of houses continued to be built with few if any windows, there was a general movement toward allowing outside light in. (Glass had been available in the area since before the community was settled, and many older residents knew how to construct sashes.) Tandy Slone, for example, had only one window in his house (No. 2), but his son Adam put two in the first hewn-log room he built (No. 4). Adam's son Green had two windows in the first room of his original house (No. 18) and put two more in the addition. When Green built his second house (No. 30), he included two in the east room and one in the west, and later turned the rear doorways into windows. There were no windows in the log section of the Isaac Caudill House (No. 7), but the later-built box kitchen had two. Jasper Caudill moved from his first house (No. 20) with few windows into the John B. Slone House (No. 6) with even fewer. He soon had three in the log room, installed three in the front box room, and put four along the rear addition (No. 28). Austin Slone lived temporarily in a house with one window (No. 33) while building his own house (No. 39), which had eight. Wiley and Ada Caudill moved out of their dark house (No. 19) to Ohio. When they returned in 1947, they built a new home (No. 42) with only one window for two rooms. When remodeling began the next year, however, picture windows were put all the way across the front. Ada's explanation for the large windows was that "I hated a dark house."[27] Many others must have, too.[28] When it came time for the community to build the schoolhouse, eight large windows were included. It may often have been necessary for children to read by the light of the coal fire or oil lamp at home,[29] but the school was built with the intention of providing much natural illumination.

A significant change in chimney placement first began to occur around the turn of the century and rapidly gained acceptance afterward. Chimneys for wood-burning fireplaces in double-pens throughout the area were nearly always on the ends of the house,[30] a practice closely followed in the Head.[31] In about 1903, however, Adam Slone added a room to his house (No. 4), but instead of building a chimney at the end of the new pen, he took down the original chimney and reas-

sembled it between the rooms, adding a second firebox. Eleven years later his son Green added a room to his house (No. 18), fully prepared to build a second chimney on the gable end of the new addition. After the room was completed, though, he canceled plans for the chimney and installed a stove at that end instead, burning coal rather than wood.

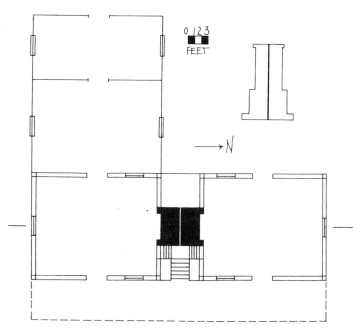

Figure 102. THE WILLIAM P. OWENS HOUSE.

People in the Head had long known of coal, but when the coal agents walked the paths between 1904 and 1905, buying mineral rights,[32] the residents' awareness of it increased dramatically. Old-timers like Tandy Slone flatly refused to burn the dirty stuff anytime during their long lives. Younger men, though, saw things differently. When Jasper Caudill, for example, remodeled John B. Slone's house, he opened the back of the north wood-burning chimney and installed a coal grate to heat the new box room. There was naturally a transitional period for such a fundamental shift in chimney design and placement, which explains why Adam Slone moved his chimney to the middle of his house before John D. Slone (No. 11) built his on the ends.

Despite the saddlebag chimney's long history in Appalachia, it evolved late in Hollybush and along Upper Caney. For some local builders the formation of the central chimney may have developed in stages. For example, the central chimney in the William P. Owen house (Fig. 102) in Trace demonstrates how two end

Figure 103. A SANDSTONE CHIMNEY, CIRCA 1900.

chimneys may have found themselves blended into a single stack with two fireboxes. When Owens moved into Trace sometime between 1895 and 1905, the right-hand room and chimney were already standing. Owens soon built the left room, mirroring the right, but instead of opening the rear of the existing chimney, he built an exact facsimile of it complete with stack, backing it up to the original one. Granted, this house demonstrated his strong desire for symmetry and balance, but the double stack also suggests that he may not yet have been able to conceive of the chimneys as a single unified piece. Before that observation could be made by him and other area builders, certain logical steps—like this double stack—needed to be built, pondered by observers, and then cognitively restructured. Later, when ready to build their own chimneys, the observers' incorporation of this restructuring resulted in a functional, unified stack that saved time, labor, and materials when compared to either double stacks or end chimneys. Many builders in the Head soon saw both this new design and reasoning as fitting into their own architectural plans.[33]

Builders like Adam and Green Slone hedged their bets on fuel at first by constructing fireboxes large enough to burn wood, even though they later used coal. As coal became increasingly accepted, modifications were made in these large fireboxes. Thin sandstone slabs were squared and mortared with clay into the box, narrowing it down to both accept the coal grate and force heat out into the room (see Fig. 15). Once that was done, wood could no longer be burned. The eight modified fireboxes known[34] are evidence of the steadily growing acceptance of coal. Later-built double fireboxes were constructed only 1½ to 2 feet wide, as opposed to the 4-foot width of the older ones, and burned only coal.[35]

As chimneys moved to the center of the house and became smaller, construction techniques also changed. The older end chimneys were built of thin sandstone pieces cut into neat rectangles and carefully stacked.[36] The time spent and the quality of workmanship are obvious (Fig. 103). The only central chimneys made of this material were those that had originally been on a gable end and later had a room added around them.[37] All subsequent central chimneys, beginning in around 1920, were built of either sandstone split into large, unfinished blocks (Fig. 104)[38] or irregularly sized creek and field rocks (Fig. 105),[39] with little regard for hard rectangular lines. The advantage of the older style of chimney was that it was durable and demonstrated the careful attitude of the builder toward his source of heat. The later styles, using larger stones less carefully shaped, were easier to erect and took much less time.

Figure 104. A BLOCK CHIMNEY, CIRCA 1940.

Figure 105. A ROCK CHIMNEY BUILT IN 1935.

The use of cement, popularly substituted for clay beginning with World War II, hastened the process even more.

These changes reflected the growing attitude among Head builders that it was important to construct quickly rather than to labor over appearances. At one time builders were willing to spend large segments of time in construction and felt comfortable doing so; the quality of their work demonstrates that. But by the 1920s the builder's time began to be regarded as better spent on other tasks. A chimney built of large blocks instead of thin, shaped slabs still conducted smoke up and out of the room. Techniques and skills were considered acceptable now if the house or outbuilding served the family for which it was built; its term of usefulness was no longer expected to stretch into the next century.

There were spatial changes as well as temporal and technical ones. Informants observed that the early settlers either cooked in the main log room or had a separate kitchen connected by a covered walkway,[40] reducing the chances of having a kitchen fire burn down the entire house. By the early 1920s, however, the kitchen began to be attached to the main room.[41] These additions were not on equal footing, structurally or functionally, with the room added along the front, though. The new front room was intended to absorb much of the family's living, sleeping, and other activities, and normally duplicated the original room in size, materials, and construction.[42] The addition built on the rear (or occasionally the front) was smaller, made of lesser-grade materials (usually riven or milled boards), and intended for the preparation of food, a task that continued to be separated from other indoor activities. Cooking in the main room became disconcerting enough for Boss and Zona Slone that they moved the cookstove out of their one-room house (No. 33) onto the porch.[43] Families slept in every room but the kitchen,[44] and when company arrived—even if the house had only one main room—they normally doubled up rather than sleep where the food was prepared. If a rainy day forced all the family inside, rarely did anyone work in the kitchen unless that work was related to food, even if the quilting frame was lowered from the ceiling and they were tripping over it.[45]

The practice of constructing additions of riven and then milled boards continued to reduce the time and energy once put into building a house. The square footage of Tandy Slone's house (No. 2), built of large poplar logs, was 400 square feet. In the late 1930s Golden Slone's house (No. 32), with its small, round-log room and rear box addition, was 426 square feet. It had slightly more living space, including the now obligatory separated kitchen, and required far less work to construct.

House positioning also shifted. Originally houses faced the direction of incoming traffic which, because of mountain paths, did not necessarily move up the hollow. Tandy Slone's house, for example, faced up the first branch because people originally came into the Head from Trace rather than up Hollybush Creek. Around the turn of the century, however, the number of well-traveled paths increased, and houses were positioned not perpendicular but parallel to the walkway.[46] The reason for this change in positioning had much to do with both the increased population and the degree of socialization. As the branches filled, the path no longer merely came up to a house but generally ran past it, often over the mountain into the next hollow, meaning that traffic now had the potential of moving both ways. To face one direction meant cutting off the view from the other. As the Head changed from "timber land" to a community, the pressure to be social and to present a certain openness increased. The house that faced the path implied that the builder and his family were willing to communicate, to be part of a cohesive group. The front of the house and its porch became symbols of open egalitarianism. Keep in mind that roads and paths in other regions generally ran past private property. In the Head the path ran through it and became its own form of social control: it would not have been wise for a person to become antagonistic with a family whose land he needed to walk through and by whose house he needed to travel in order to get to his own. Moreover, facing the path did not show the suspicion that facing down the path suggested.

Once accepted, this form of architectural politeness was followed scrupulously, even in extreme cases. Golden Slone's last house (No. 32), despite being tightly nested into the head of the second branch, faced the path where it nearly dead-ended at a hillside wall. The houses on the north side of the third branch all faced the path,[47] even though positioning them higher up the hill and swinging them east would have provided a better view and more sun. Instead, most sat in the shade and faced the opposite dark hillside, indications of the strength of prevailing social graces and of curiosity about who moved up and down the road.

One architectural rule that apparently evolved from the frontal presentation was the minimal mixing of materials along side-by-side rooms. A log room could be next to a log room, even though one might be round and the other hewn, but log next to box was not approved; it appeared to be outside the occupants' aesthetic realm.[48] As milled lumber became increasingly available and box rooms were added along the fronts of houses—creating material dissimilarities—the log walls still visible were covered with clapboarding so that the frontal materials were uniform in appearance. This

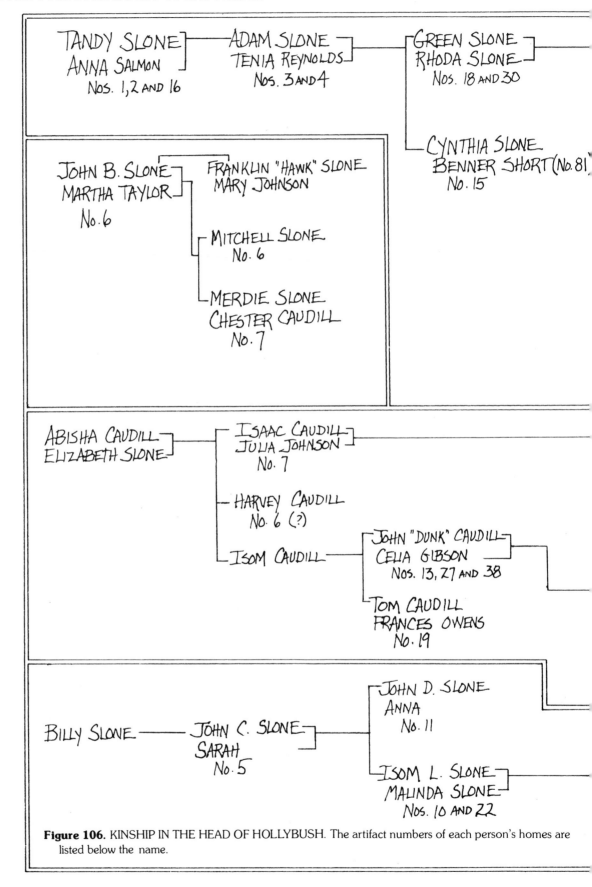

Figure 106. KINSHIP IN THE HEAD OF HOLLYBUSH. The artifact numbers of each person's homes are listed below the name.

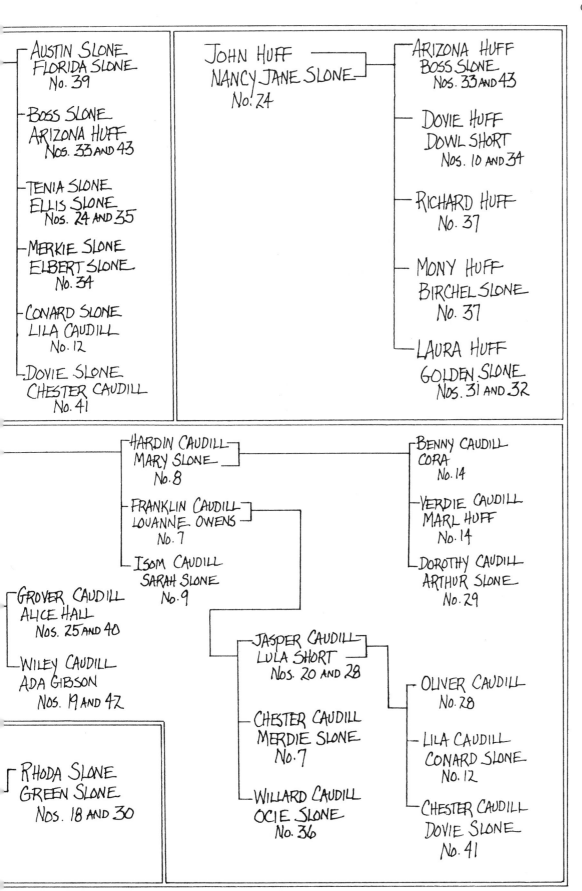

intimated a changing attitude toward milled lumber. Although readily used, it was at first considered an inferior material and relegated to the rear of the house; additional front rooms were still built of logs because they suggested both an adherence to tradition and a preference for strong, suitable material where passersby could most easily see it. The increased use of box along the front in the late 1930s and early 1940s[49] coincides with its popularization as a component not only for additions but for entire houses.

Property division (Fig. 106) among Head residents was handled one of two ways: early settlers, like Tandy Slone and John C. Slone, sold part of their holdings to others who wished to move in. The original holdings of each then shrank to about half, from approximately two hundred acres to one hundred.[50] As the years passed, however, many of the children of these first settlers grew to maturity, and provision needed to be made for them. Although Tandy moved out, his son Adam stayed and had two children who lived in the Head as adults. John C. Slone also had two; Isaac Caudill, not in the first wave of settlement, had four; Hardin Caudill, three. Children who intended to remain in the Head were each allotted about twenty acres for their own use. Legal transfer usually took place, if at all, only when these children wished to leave. For example, no record can be found that Adam Slone transferred the property allotted to his daughter Cynthia (No. 15) to either her or her husband, Benner Short. A site was provided for them and a house built, but the land was not legally conveyed, remaining instead in the hands of the patriarch. Normally, however, when the children needed cash to move to another area, the land was transferred to them and then sold. The patriarchs' individual holdings would by this time have shrunk to twenty-five to fifty acres.

John and Nancy Jane Huff's property history lends insight into how these assignments worked. In 1925 they purchased nearly the entire second branch from Isom L. Slone, who inherited it from his father, John C. Slone. John and Nancy Jane moved in with four daughters and one son and built a house (No. 24) considered large enough for them all. Within ten years, however, the children had grown up and were marrying. Arizona married Boss Slone, Green's son, and settled in the first branch (No. 33). Dovie, Mony, and Laura married men from the outside who all moved into the Head for a time. Dovie and her husband, Dowl Short, were allotted property in the head of the branch (No. 34) in about 1934.[51] Mony and her husband, Birchel Slone, were given land (No. 37) across the creek from John and Nancy Jane in 1942.[52] Laura and her husband, Golden Slone, were allotted two separate

sections, first toward the mouth of the branch (No. 31) and then up in the head (No. 32). When they moved out in the late 1930s, the plot they had lived on was still controlled by John Huff and was later rented to James and Lillie Huff for one-third of the corn they raised. Mony and Birchel left the Head in the early 1940s, and her brother Richard moved into their home, staying a year or so. When Dowl and Dovie wanted to leave Hollybush in 1944, their property was finally transferred to them, ten years after they moved onto it.[53] John and Nancy themselves moved out in 1945, selling much of the property to Ellis Slone and transferring part to Arizona,[54] their only remaining child in the Head.

Once land had been allotted to children, shelters needed to be erected and a pattern of housing developed, based on relative community social position. Houses that first- and second-wave settlers built were large enough to shelter the extended family, but those built for newly married children were constructed with different specifications in mind. These "offspring houses" nearly all followed the same basic plan: a small log room averaging about 16 feet square, with a rear box addition, a front porch, and three doorways—one in the center of each long wall front to back (see No. 15, for example). The offspring house was not simply a popular style freely adapted, but was rather based on caste. For example, workings were organized in 1935 to build houses for both Green Slone and his son-in-law, Ellis Slone. Neighbors and relatives gathered to help both men, but Green was the recipient of a large, two-room hewn house (No. 30); Ellis's was a single round-log room with a riven board kitchen, built in one day (No. 35). Once the help had been assembled, Ellis, with some added effort, could have had a house equal to Green's, but that would have upset unarticulated community rules. Green was an adult whose established position in the community befitted a large house. Ellis and his wife Tenia were just starting their adult lives and were not seen as needing or deserving more than their small round-log house. Theirs was regarded as an adequate structure for the young and as yet childless couple; it symbolized both their status in the community and the fact that their producing years were still ahead of them. John Huff's house (No. 24) consisted of two large hewn-log rooms and an addition. He and his family were considered to need this amount of living space, but his house also reflected his age, experience, and vast acreage.[55] None of his children had such a fine structure built for them, nor did they expect it, for they understood the social and architectural rules.

Newlyweds comprehended that as their spatial requirements increased, as with the birth of children, the basic structure could be added to.[56] Of the fourteen houses with this general floor plan, twelve[57] were known to have been built for people whose parents were already established in the Head. The system was predicated on actual rather than imagined need; there was no point in building more rooms than were regarded as necessary. Juxtapose this with the more modern concept of suburban couples earmarking the "baby's room" before an actual pregnancy has occurred. The need is anticipated, and professional architects take these demographics and yearnings into account; they are careful to insert that architectural space. The buyers will grow into the house; if the baby does not arrive, a television or sewing machine can be moved in, providing a new function for the room. These concepts did not apply in the Head, however. When the size of a family had grown enough to warrant additional space, a working was organized and a new room erected, based on observable need. The available building resources and the ability to handle construction by means of the manpower and skills within the community made this outlook and approach possible. It would be unfair to say that Hollybush builders never took the future into account, but they dealt with the immediate, rather than the all-encompassing, future. Planning for the future may have been psychologically comforting but was not reason enough to create sheltered space for things not immediately within reach. When Tandy and Anna Slone "retired" to Adam's farm, a one-room, round-log house (No. 16) was built for them, a decision based on the needs of two elderly people without dependents; aging had changed their position in the community. Where once they had warranted more—by virtue of their experience, their vitality, and the number of children they had reared—they now warranted less, much like a newlywed couple. Tandy and Anna had come full circle.

When Conard and Lila Slone (Jasper Caudill's daughter) were married in 1950, they moved into and remodeled the John C. Slone House (No. 12), tearing down the north room (12ii) and building a rear box kitchen (12iii)—thus duplicating the house's original offspring floor plan. Even though the north room could have been repaired and retained, the old rules appeared too strong to resist. They had to tear it down and comply, and at the end of their labors they had the type of house the community would have built for them in a working—if such a practice had not by then been long abandoned.

Building for a predicated need was eventually recognized; for example, by the mid-1950s one of the few remaining residents in the Head built a barn based on his imagined needs. The community was rapidly being deserted, with no new occupants taking over old places, yet Boss Slone built a four-stall barn (No. 61) with little in the way of outside help. Agriculture was dwindling because of the declining outside market, yet he planned for the "future" by building a structure his needs could grow into—crops he would plant and stock he would buy. But by 1960 the future was dead. Boss moved to Hindman, leaving this structure as testament to the incompatibility of these diametric systems, one based on the observable present and the other on the imagined future.

The most telling architectural change was the increased fragmentation of house space. In early one-room houses, family activity took place in a single chamber—cooking, food preservation, the preparation of fabric for clothing, haircuts, patching cuts and bruises, courtship, children's games, adult conversation, music, tales, sleeping, and on and on. As single-pens were transformed into double-pens and saddlebags, the family was allowed to expand its perimeters somewhat. Sleeping and general activities took place in one room, and cooking and dining in the other, meaning that the majority of the family's indoor time was still spent together in one room.

By 1930, additions were being attached to double-pens and saddlebags. Cooking and eating shifted to these additions, allowing family activity to spread out. Some members slept in one room, designated a bedroom, and the remainder slept in the other, designated the "settin' room."

Interior partitions began appearing in the early 1940s. The east room of Green Slone's house (No. 30) was made into two uncomfortably small bedrooms by a milled-board partition; the front room of Dowl Short's house (No. 34), measuring 16 by 17 feet, was partitioned. Family members were beginning to separate themselves from one another. When Chester Caudill (see No. 7) died in 1947, his widow, deciding that her daughters should have a room separate from the rest of the family, hired Boss Slone to build a box bedroom for them. When Jasper Caudill remodeled his house (No. 28), he added not only the large front room but also three small rooms to the rear—a kitchen, a dining room, and a bedroom for one or two of his sons. Wiley and Ada Caudill (see No. 42), Grover Caudill (No. 40), and Benny Caudill (No. 14) all turned their small saddlebags into four-room houses, further fragmenting living space as they did so.

The family living in one room had to coexist, and oral testimony suggests it did.[58] Naturally, there was subjugation of individual will for the sake of the group. The ability to get along was paramount, and argumentative tendencies were best kept in check. Only outdoors could a family member find solitude. The increased number of rooms and partitions in houses meant that there was a growing emphasis on and recognition of the individual. Children separated from the remainder of the family by an interior wall, if only at night or when they sought more private moments, were being encouraged to cope in a changing society where individual initiative needed to be relied upon more than community action. Austin Slone's house (No. 39), built in the mid-1940s, was not much bigger than John C. Slone's (No. 5), built in about 1890; where John's was one large room, though, Austin's was five. Austin knew of the large one-room alternative, but he reasoned, "I wanted more rooms even if they were smaller."[59] His reaction was only natural, considering all that had happened to his community.

5. The Reasons for Change

The center of cultural logic had shifted. The community's sense of obligation toward itself had been supplanted by an obligation more narrowly defined, despite a long-held cooperative tradition in Hollybush. On the day Tandy Slone built his first pole house, he had help, even though he and his family were moving into the Head alone. Informants question only whether it was the Shorts or another family who came in over Trace and aided Tandy in building both this and his second home. After Isaac Caudill, Adam Slone, John C. Slone, and their respective families moved into this newly established area, a system of mutual aid was adopted, patterned on similar systems in the region. Men, women, and children would gather for a specified period in what was called a "working" to aid a neighbor or relative in a task that might be physically impossible, or be regarded as taking too long, for the family to do alone. Two frequent examples were the caring of fields and the construction of shelter.

Once crops had sprouted, residents first weeded one family's fields and then moved on to another farm the next dry day, continuing until each cooperating farmer's land was taken care of. Work loads were thought to have averaged out. Each family obviously benefited when they needed help, but they were expected to return help in kind. The advantage of spending two weeks hoeing other people's fields when it would have taken a single family two weeks to hoe its own was the sense of fellowship, the psychological comfort of knowing they belonged and could count on their neighbors in good times and bad.

One of the most moving examples of this fellowship happened when the community was beginning to break up in the late 1940s; it represents one of the last occurrences of the "working" system. One member contracted cancer and was operated on in faraway Huntington, West Virginia. His prognosis was poor, and he wished to return home. His neighbors met the ambulance, which returned him as far as the mouth of Trace, with a wagon full of pillows so he could rest easily. They pulled the wagon, at an easy pace to make him as comfortable as possible, up Trace and over the mountain, each man helping to brake the wheels on the descent into the first branch by hanging onto the spokes, careful to move slowly and ease the invalid's discomfort. When he died, his neighbors built his coffin and carried him to his grave. Another informant warmly recalled that in the working system, "no matter what the situation was or what kind of crisis it would be . . . neighbors would just pitch in and help them do whatever needed to be done."[1]

In construction, men with practiced skills used their knowledge to notch logs, split roof shingles, and build fireboxes and chimneys. The less accomplished did as they were told, saw that materials were at hand, and perhaps learned something. Mary Sparkman recalled her mother's memories of Head workings where "all the kids, they worked young, you know. They learned to build houses and all stuff. Everybody pitched in and helped. . . . Whole families would come in and help."[2] Another informant explained where perhaps some of their energy came from: "They'd have their booze and they'd all get to drinking, and they'd put up a house; every bit of it got put up. There would be maybe ten or fifteen men, some sawing, some hammering."[3] Women provided the meals, cooking most of the day at the recipients' home.

A single family alone could not, without extreme difficulty, gather, hew, notch, and hoist the massive logs that tradition called for. As long as the working system survived, so did the older building techniques, since they reinforced each other. Large houses and carefully shaped logs were the expected results of a large work force whose members considered such activity good use of their time. When they stepped back and viewed the results, the well-built house constructed along traditional lines and by traditional techniques was the visual and emotional reward for their cooperative effort. Tradition could easily be maintained under such conditions.

One disadvantage of such a ready work force was that it depressed the price that physical labor could bring, a fact that became more noticeable as these people began to value the transfer of cash rather than goods. Labor in the Head prior to 1920 brought 75¢ to $1.00 a day for men and women, and 50¢ for children. Some of the few jobs available were building fences, hoeing corn, and clearing fields. All were done for cash if performed for outsiders, since the money could be used to buy some of the few early consumer goods available. If performed for Head residents, the tasks were usually absorbed into the working system or repaid by labor in kind.

Even though the Head economy by today's standards would have been called depressed, the mutual reliance the people exercised meant that many of their basic needs were well provided for. Each family raised enough corn to make corn bread and to feed the stock and poultry and maintained one or two vegetable gardens to supply greens; the cow supplied the dairy products; the hogs, the meat. When someone was sick, he could call on any of four women in the Head who were regarded as "herb" women: Frances Caudill, Tom's wife; Nancy Jane Huff; Martha Slone, wife of John B.; and Celia Caudill, Dunk's spouse. Each one knew, for example, how to mix ingredients like camphor shavings, kerosene, and the juices from a baked onion in the proper proportions to treat virus and pneumonia in children: placed in a cloth bag, the mixture was tied around the sick child's neck with a string. Other illnesses were taken care of in the home with less specialized care. A mixture of corn whiskey, ginger, and honey was thought to prevent disease if taken every day. A chest cold could be combatted by rubbing warm groundhog grease over the sufferer's chest and back. When not needed for medicinal purposes, groundhog grease was used to waterproof boots in winter and to preserve the mule's leather harnesses.

If some people in the Head made medicines, others took care of such tasks as pulling teeth, building pine caskets, or cutting hair for their neighbors. Hawk Slone was the dentist, armed with pliers and whiskey; Jasper Caudill built caskets; and Chester Caudill (No. 7) was the local barber. Chester provided his services on Sunday afternoons—indoors if it was wintertime or raining, and outdoors in the yard in pleasant weather. Chester also made gunstocks for his neighbors, which were often traded for cured hams. Delivering babies was the job of the local midwife, Frances Caudill, who by the 1930s began charging for her services. Ellis Slone recalled the birth of his son:

It costed me anywhere from $2.00 to $3.00, and that was a lot of money then to spend for a kid to be born. [This fee was also payable in cured hams instead of cash.] She [Ellis's wife, Tenia] was hoeing corn, and I was working off, hoeing corn at another place [outside the Head for cash], and they sent and got me that night. She led the field, a whole bunch hoeing corn; it was our corn and I was working off and they was helping her [a communal hoeing where Tenia led the procession of workers and set the pace]. She worked all day, and he was born that night.[4]

Since the Head was a community where people were dependent on each other, outsiders were viewed with suspicion. Ellis Slone also noted that "you didn't let anybody come in, an outsider, if he didn't belong. That fellow stated his business and why he was there; it's not like it is now; you may go out here [on Caney Creek] and not know who your neighbor is; you just move in and move out, and you never know him. Back then everybody knowed each other."[5]

It was this sense of knowing each other, this sense of community, that worked itself into the prevailing attitude they once held toward their architecture. Retrospectively, informants feel that the log architecture was better than the later box type because it was warmer in winter and cooler in summer. It also reflected shared values that informants now look upon with longing. The interdependency of families gave community members a sense of understanding the structure of their lives and a feeling of fitting into a controlled and comprehensible system. Cooperation maintained community. Time spent in helping each other hoe, tend the sick, and—in particular—build was time that was regarded as well used. A straight-edged hewn log would better shed water, making the log more durable; a complex notch gave the building stability at the corners. An added reason to hew and notch, though, was that the builders had the time, and shaping logs was seen as an ambitious way to spend it.

Every cultural group must distinguish between relative values of time. Some tasks are deemed exceedingly worthwhile, and others are not. Benjamin

Franklin's adage about being "useful and good" fits well into contemporary western standards of industrious behavior. Today, time spent toward career advancement is considered a worthy application of the hours and minutes. On the other hand, young adults sitting in the movies each afternoon and vicariously experiencing life cause mothers to worry because their time is not seen as being properly applied. The same distinctions existed in the Head. Hewing logs and carefully working the notches was deemed time well spent, time that the participants could relate to with pride at the end of the day. When the result of an organized working was a house built with the obvious care and craftsmanship of the John B. Slone House (No. 6), for example, it stood as a positive symbol for the community and the cooperative tenets upon which its members had based their small society. It was the physical and visual evidence of their efforts, their care, and the days and hours they were willing to dedicate. A circle of reinforced values formed. The more time put into shaping the logs, the better they were considered to look, since some positive attribute must be found in handmade objects, besides sheer utilitarianism, to justify the action it takes to create them. The pleasure of looking at and feeling the smooth well-shaped logs encouraged future expenditures of time for like tasks. The longevity of these houses also became a positive and admired trait, one equated with craftsmanship and its prerequisite of pledged time, the accepted and expected catalyst.

This logic also applied to outbuildings and even chimneys. A hewn-log barn or crib demonstrated how the builder and community arranged priorities and structured their days. Care in building was important enough to postpone other activities. There was no urgency to be done in a day in order to return hurriedly to another and seemingly more important task. The logs in John B. Slone's corncrib (No. 46) are a testament to the community's past values, as are the thin chimney stones used in the older homes, where each slab was carefully worked into the required, measured shape.

An analysis dependent on the notion that these farmers had little else to do in no way explains their choice. This is a critical point—they had a choice. They could have apportioned their time differently and placed more value upon other activities. Those thin chimney stones state, loudly, that they did not work quickly in order to rest or to move on to another duty; instead, they worked slowly because the results and the pleasure of careful performance carried their own reward. If they had not, all chimneys would have looked like the roughly worked one in Green Slone's second house (No. 30) instead of like those in John B. Slone's or Isaac Caudill's (Nos. 6 and 7), built thirty-five to forty years earlier. The alteration of chimney workmanship and

materials to fit into compressed schedules dramatically evinces how the conception of time and its useful application had changed in Hollybush. Time was now obviously being spent on matters considered more important, matters concerned with the total reshaping of the Head's economic system.

Ideas of how time should be assigned began changing in the 1890s when the lumber merchants showed these people that natural resources, like certain hardwoods, were worth cash. The introduction of abundant specie and the realization that the surrounding hillsides, which were being cleared for planting anyway, had monetary value had a profound effect on the local cultural system. When the coal merchants began blanketing the area in the early 1900s, the conceptual connections between money and natural resources had already been well established, but coal made itself even more promising. Not only was cash paid for mineral rights, but there was the assurance of steady work to those who would travel to the faraway mines and dig the fuel for northern industries. Trees in a hollow could be cut down only once every thirty years; coal could be harvested unceasingly. This knowledge brought about not only a changing concept of time in Hollybush, but also a new acceptance of technology and consumerism, as profound an acceptance as that elsewhere of the triangular sail, the water mill, steam power, electricity. The acceptance of coal forever transformed this small, isolated society.

A critical question arises: why did a potential cash system and promises of outside employment look so attractive to these people who had, for generations, lived so differently? What was it that caused this agrarian society to listen, however faintly, to the beckonings of industrialism? We have all become so enmeshed in the achievements and failings of technology that we neglect to realize that in the not-so-distant past alternatives were possible for some groups, and that the acceptance of technology and consumerism was predicated on choice as well as gradual conditioning. Many societies, particularly in America, embraced with passion whatever increased productivity and saved time. People in the Head became increasingly aware that they could maintain old ways but chose instead to gradually accept the alternative. (That gradual acceptance helps to explain why the older building techniques in the Head overlapped with newer ones instead of falling away in neat stages. Benny Caudill, for example, was not particularly interested in demonstrating the older concepts of time well spent when he built a box house [No. 14] in 1915. Yet Arthur Slone, who helped build his own hewn saddlebag [No. 29] across the road from Benny twenty years later, was interested in the past, or at least gave it tacit approval, when he allowed his father to hew and notch the logs. John C. Slone built a round-log barn [No. 44] before 1900, but Green Slone built a hewn-log crib [No. 58] for his son-in-law in the mid-1940s, about the same time that he built a riven board crib for himself.)

I have not answered the questions posed because I do not know the answers. Jacob Bronowski called this steady movement toward the acceptance of technology the "ascent of man."[6] But Henry Adams interpreted the same movement quite differently; he saw Western culture as leaving the humanistic influence of the Virgin to embrace the mechanistic influence of what he called the Dynamo. It was Henry who warned us "that Radium denied its God."[7] The consensual answer among Hollybush informants, explaining their move toward industrialism as an "easier" life, may be the correct one despite its unpretentiousness. Mining coal was considered less arduous than hoeing corn, and a steady paycheck was its own form of security. Perhaps the weightier (and still unanswered) questions are these: why do cultures, in their collective move toward ease, so readily sacrifice their humanness as the considered cost? Why, within a culture, is the ability of individuals to share with each other quickly accepted as the inherent trait most expendable? This pattern of embracing new ways at great cultural cost repeated itself in Hollybush, with its emerging cash economy.

Work in the mines was at first thought too distant for men in the Head: the closest ones, in Wayland and Lackey, were half a day's ride by wagon down the Caney Road and up along Beaver Creek. The mines initially exerted influence over Head residents by making it known that they would buy, for cash, any extra produce grown in these remote agricultural settlements for their company stores. These supplies were then sold to miners, many of whom had left their communities to live in company housing and were no longer able to provide their own sustenance. The Siren's call was answered, and the system of selling the extras, called "peddling," caused additional fields to be cleared and crops planted. It also brought to the Head both cash and consumerism. Men who delivered produce once a week had the opportunity to look at all the wonders that were steadily spreading out from the coal towns.

By the late 1920s the desire for cash and the things it could buy became urgent enough that some men in the Head were willing to work in the mines by staying in Wayland or Lackey all week. They left Hollybush on Sunday afternoons and walked or hitched rides, slept in company housing with men in similar circumstances, and returned home late Friday night. Wives and children were expected to perform their agrarian duties as best they could.[8] When the northern factories began

recruitment drives in the 1930s, many men went to work in the Michigan and Ohio areas at six-month intervals, leaving their families behind, since their objective was to save as much and spend as little as possible. They would depart in the fall and return in time for spring planting, a cyclical process repeated by many until the mid-1940s.

Also in the mid-1940s, a three-mile-long road was finally built over Caney Mountain, connecting with Route 80, the largest road through Knott County, and leading directly to Lackey. This meant that men could walk more easily from Caney, catch rides to the mines, and return at day's end—thus saving the money once spent on company housing, but necessitating either staying on Caney with a relative during the week or leaving the Head at 3:00 A.M. in order to get to the mines on time. One informant recalled his transportation method: "I'd walk. Plenty of times I've walked from the Head of Hollybush to Bob Waddell's place, you know over here, and catch a truck to load coal. I believe I have left at two or three o'clock in the morning, and I'd get in at eight, nine, ten o'clock at night. But I still worked."[9] The key phrase here is "I still worked," which implies that staying in the Head and working at farming would not have carried the same importance that working in the mines did. Time was increasingly seen as better spent on outside employment.

As men were being drawn out of the Head, even if only on a daily basis, community self-reliance rapidly began to wane. A store (No. 71) that opened in the 1930s not only met community needs but helped satisfy the new demand for consumer goods invading the area—not for the first time, since backpack peddlers carrying small merchandise had made their way through the mountains for years, but now in a steady and fast-flowing stream. Once cash became more plentiful in eastern Kentucky, retail merchants began supplying goods and dreams. Cloth in pretty patterns, factory tools, candy, furniture, and coal stoves quickly became available.

The renewable supplies and the occasional new item, like potted meat, made it continually clear that there was something new under the sun and made some traditional activities, like curing pork, a little more expendable. Reliance could be placed on someone else, somewhere outside the Head; the anonymous commercial manufacturer was somehow entrusted to provide selected clothing and food items. The stores and the men who ran them, Green Slone and Jasper Caudill, were caught between the two systems—one communal and the other consumerist. Their efforts made it possible for the community to continue to exist in increasingly apparent isolation by eliminating the necessity of traveling great distances to trade. But the stores, while being convenient, continued to bring about the inevitable. They whetted the residents' growing appetite for goods and conveniences and eventually helped destroy the community and system they were intended to serve; when Jasper moved and Green died, the dependence on commercial goods had grown to such a degree that many people felt compelled to move out and be nearer to other stores.

Consider also the impact of magazines and catalogs. Put up to insulate walls and improve appearances, they continually and visually presented the promises of the consumer-oriented and industrial society; their pages depicted not coal miners and traditional farmers, but suburban men who carried undented lunch boxes to clean factories, wearing polished work boots and pressed work clothes. Their wives had well-equipped white kitchens, and their children every kind of toy. The images of factory-made furniture, lawn chairs, automobile upholstery, and electric refrigerators constantly beckoned to people in the Head as examples of industrial wonders and conveniences. Residents could state their dreams by using these same pages and giving prominence on the wall to their particular choices of symbolic images. The problem was that these longings were not being expressed in traditional symbols like ballad verse but in symbols conceived of by national advertisers. Rather than turn their backs on such temptations and embrace the relative security and comfort of their communal system, residents cupped their ears to the wooings of merchandising. This was not an overnight occurrence, but rather a slow realization of and move toward what would be considered the "mainstream" of American life. It coincides with the altering of many of the traditional patterns and practices in their lives.

The personal manufacture of cloth and clothing, for example, which had once taken up much of a woman's time, became a product of the past, for the catalogs and stores now supplied this need. One informant recalled her grandparents' descriptions of making their own clothing from flax and wool: homemade clothing designated as "good" was worn little and passed down through the family when the original wearer died; Work clothing was repeatedly patched because of the difficulty of spinning and weaving new cloth. "I heard my grandparents talk about weaving and making their own blankets and knitting their own socks and making lots of clothing, but now I never seen none of it myself,"[10] she recalled. If that informant, in her early seventies, had not seen any clothes made in the traditional way, then those skills would have begun to be replaced with an alternative system about the time of the coal industry's

permanent entrance into eastern Kentucky, between 1890 and 1910. The time lag in the Head of Hollybush would have put the change there at an even later date. By the 1930s clothes were being made in Knott County from "factory"—the local term for commercially produced cloth. The knowledge needed to create fabric from regional substances had been displaced by the availability of bulk cloth sold in the county seat.

The mercantile economy had also begun to make Head residents more transient, particularly in the third branch. Wiley and Ada Caudill, for example, lived in the Head for three separate periods. Wiley grew up on the branch, yet he and his wife established a pattern of moving out when he worked in the mines and in when he did not (their sudden departure after the shooting incident in 1940 [see No. 19] was, of course, a deviation from this pattern). Tandy Slone had also been transient years earlier, but he always stayed within the same communal / agrarian system regardless of where he lived. When Wiley or his contemporaries moved out, they shifted not only geographically but also culturally, from a farming to an industrial system. Returning for the last time from northern Ohio, Wiley and Ada brought some of its suburban architectural trappings with them: picture windows, the horizontal ranch look, and simulated-stone tar paper covering the three sides of their log house (No. 42) observable from the road. For them, the industrial system seemed too harsh. They were willing to hedge their bets and present the well-to-do facade of the suburban household in an area that still possessed some of the comforting logic and values ultimately more important to them.

This change in systematic emphasis throughout the Head also brought about an eclipse of visual orderliness in architecture. Hewn logs once had positive values of care and time attached to them. These sentiments softened as more structures were built of round logs or riven boards. The ascent of the new style was dependent on the descending value of the old. When Boss Slone said the round logs in his house (No. 43) would last as long as hewn ones, he believed it. Concepts of longevity had changed: it was not necessary for his house or his outbuildings to last longer than his own planned use for them. Ellis Slone best summed up the primary advantage of round logs when he said, "They was easier and quicker. Get my house built and I could get in it quicker."[11]

On the rare occasions when logs were still hewn, speed became a primary objective. Conard Slone assumed the north room of his house (No. 12) to have been built later than the south room, not because it looked older, but because the logs were poorly shaped. Quality in construction and an era in time had been equated. If a log was poorly crafted, it was because the once traditional allotment of time had dwindled, an occurrence beginning in the Head around 1930. When Tom Caudill built the east room of his house (No. 19) in about 1918, hewing logs was still seen as time well spent. When Wiley Caudill added the west room in 1937, however, time allocated to shaping logs was no longer regarded in the same light. Wiley had just returned from a stint in the mines and may have again had the time, but the tenor of life and the accepted construction methods had changed so that no one, neither he nor those helping him, wanted to hew the logs. Better to leave them round and set them up quickly.

By now men were either working outside the Head, looking for work, or worrying about finding it. Priorities had shifted, signaling the end to the old style of architecture. Time was now better spent pursuing interests and goals more in line with the "mainstream," which explains why some of the older barns and cribs were made of round logs, but few of the newer ones were hewn. The pride associated with shaping logs and with the old agrarian life style had diminished. Ellis Slone preferred to leave the Head at 3:00 A.M. to work in the mines rather than spend the day farming. Farming could be taken care of by the men in slack times, or by the women and children during the week. The male had taken on the role and pressures of the paycheck provider. When the area's economy shifted to one based on cash rather than on the exchange of goods and labor, and people's expectations moved toward the factory-made product rather than the handmade one, a young husband chasing cash jobs on the outside—however small—was considered to be making better use of his time than if he had stayed on his small farm. He was better off selling extra produce to the community center on Caney Creek[12] or trying again to work for the gas company, which temporarily needed men to clear away trees for the laying of pipe. When another crib was needed, he found it easier and more expedient to build it of either round logs or riven boards than to do it the old way.

For one important outbuilding, the smokehouse, box became the preferred material. There may have been a slower acceptance of milled boards in house construction, since box was initially thought not substantial enough for human shelter. Boards were quickly adopted for smokehouses, though, where less strength was required, because they went up quickly; and the cash necessary for purchase was fast becoming available. Although not as long-lasting as log, box kept the varmints and weather out and the smoke in just as well. Many residents quietly understood that changes were occurring in the Head and that new became old sooner

than before. But builders assessed the new material and knew that when it wore out it could be quickly replaced. Under these circumstances, men could not be bothered shaping logs as they once did; if a man persisted in hewing logs, he might have been seen as perhaps having too much time on his hands.

Workings became increasingly difficult to organize, further extending this architectural revamping. When offspring houses were first built, the community was willing to invest the time necessary to fit them into the building scheme, with uniformity in the treatment of logs and an obvious adherence to set values. But by the mid-1930s, when a working was called to construct such a house, only one day was allotted to erect it of round logs and assorted shaped creekbed stones. Ellis Slone, the occupant of an offspring house, preferred round logs. No one gave him much argument on the day his house (No. 35) was built. They were pleased to help him but also thought they had other and more important individual concerns. When another working was organized to build Golden and Laura Slone a new house (No. 32), shortly after they were burned out of their first one (No. 31), round logs were again used, reinforcing the perception that people no longer believed they had the time for workings that they once did; if they did join in, it was important to erect the building quickly. When Dowl Short built his home (No. 34) in 1935, he had only the help of his father-in-law, John Huff, and his brother-in-law, Golden Slone, whom he paid for his labor. There was no organized working to help Dowl haul the boards over from Trace and erect them. The responsibility for providing housing fell primarily on Dowl's shoulders; only his family, not his community, helped in easing the burden. Golden's first house (No. 31) was built about the same time as Dowl's, also without benefit of a working. Golden hired John Huff, who worked free, and Jake Slone, who was paid $40, to help with the hewn-log structure. Golden himself could not help, because he had taken a job in the Wayland railroad yards and was gone during the week. By paying, though, he could get the quality of house he wanted, so vestiges of the old preference still lingered. A new pattern was firmly being formed, however. A working could no longer be relied upon to supply the necessary manpower and skills. Many men were working outside the Head and could not contribute labor and know-how; they were needed elsewhere. Community members could still be counted on to help in adversity, but the quality of building had to be downgraded in order to fit into new time schedules. By the late 1930s architectural work either became a spare-time project done between outside jobs or was hired out to men with construction skills and no outside employment. No latitude was taken with traditional house designs by these new "professional" builders, though: Golden's house followed the standard offspring floor plan, and Dowl's was based on the plan of the house from which the boards were taken.

Austin Slone recalled that he "couldn't remember anybody having a working after around 1940."[13] The only reason given for the partial continuation of workings even into the late 1930s was the free time caused by the high rate of joblessness in the area. Unemployment was viewed as time not spent earning cash on the outside; farming was for food and supplemental income only. Austin also added, "You know, once there wasn't any work. If you had a working and somebody helped you, well, you knowed that you wasn't tied down to anything and you could help him back when he needed you."[14] Keep in mind that this communal system had been only partial and in no way utopic. There had sometimes been flare-ups of temper and misunderstanding, but the working concept had allowed for reliance on others, and most took from and gave to it. When men finally became tied to outside employment, workings ended, taking with them the relative security of the communal system and leaving self-reliance and individual initiative in its place.

This cultural transformation was architecturally reflected in the not-so-subtle changes that commenced to occur in log dwellings. When Grover Caudill built his house (No. 25) in the early 1920s, he positioned the chimney along the rear eave. This placement is far from rare in log housing, but when nearly everyone in the Head built chimneys on the gable ends, it took some courage to do otherwise.[15] The stated reason for the new chimney's placement was that it saved time, since the stack did not need to be as high. Perhaps it did save time, but if it was the first house in the Head to be so built, and apparently it was, it was both noticed and commented on by neighbors and passersby. Explanations were given and probably accepted, since change was being felt in Hollybush already: crops could be sold for cash, and Benny Caudill, down the hollow, had already built himself a house made only of boards (No. 14). By the time Birchel Slone built his chimney along the rear eave (No. 37), seventeen years later, passersby commented very little. Residents had become more inclined to accept design variations because of other accelerating changes: men were traveling to jobs in faraway Detroit, and promises of wonders to come were continually evident in "wish books." Soon after Birchel finished his house, he moved out of the Head in order to be nearer the main creek and cash economy. He was young and self-reliant, and his character was not well suited to straddling two systems. Perhaps it took personalities like his to vary design and move away from architectural tradition, encouraging others to modify their techniques before changing circumstances forced them to do so.

When Hawk Slone, another example, built his riven-board house (No. 23) in 1923, he demonstrated that he recognized the advantages of the new without being too emotionally tied to the old, promptly conceding to the principle of man-hours saved by utilizing an alternative form of construction. Hawk had clear objectives—he was not as concerned with light, air circulation, or separating food preparation from other work as he was with having his house quickly and inexpensively built. He felt no social pressure to build in the old way, nor was he concerned with popular style like the later adapters of boards and battens. Hawk, in all probability, saw Benny Caudill's milled-board house (No. 14), built eight years earlier, and modified that building technique to fit his own needs. Benny was a mover and shaker who had patterned his house on other box houses popping up along the larger creeks near the sawmills. The location of Benny's house, however, put him geographically closer to these new concepts being formulated outside of Hollybush. Hawk, more isolated, did not have the price of milled lumber, so he rived his boards, not just for an addition but for the entire house—a radical step. An eccentric character like Hawk first sensed the winds of change and which way a culture, crawling through the phases of traditionality, was beginning to move. He could emotionally exist outside the community even while technically living in it; he may well have understood, before his neighbors did, that one who no longer considered building in log as time well spent, for whatever reason, should exercise an alternative. Hawk's willingness to use an alternative, by moving into a box house from a hewn-log house (No. 17), is crucial to Hollybush's story: it indicates that in the early 1920s at least one person had visually admitted that the old system was being eclipsed. Even though Hawk's box house was made of riven boards and its builder was no paragon of agrarian or industrial virtue, his structure is representative of the developing overlap that would result in the sweeping transition from log to box construction.

As Boss Slone built his round-log house (No. 43), this same growing willingness to alter and to experiment enabled him to leave out an alternating front and rear door. Boss based his room sizes on tradition, but when it came time to pierce the walls, his floor plan seemed predicated only on individual concerns: the front door in the north room was omitted so that a dining table could be placed along that wall; the rear door was included for easy access to the coal pile out back; the pattern of three piercings per room, two windows and a door, was based on the premise that there should always be a nearby escape route in case of fire. Enough cultural changes had occurred that Boss and his wife Zona, not able to count on a working and its collective wisdom, found themselves building alone. They based their choices not on "the way everybody did it" (Boss's explanation for the shape and style of his hewn-log house, No. 33, built twelve years earlier)[16] but on personal preferences and observation.

Coal made its influence felt in yet another way, for the mineral not only offered jobs and new vistas of expectation, but its adaptation as a fuel intensified the awareness of the growing importance of efficiency. The iron stove, as an example, was brought into the area in the wave of coal consumerism. Many informants have commented on how they eventually accepted coal as stove fuel because of its speed in reaching high temperatures, meaning that food could be prepared more quickly. As one informant commented, "Coal heats your stove quicker, and it don't burn up as fast as wood. Now if you cook with wood, you have to just stand there and keep putting wood in, and it takes it longer to heat your stove up. But coal, put you a little coal in there, and it heats your stove a lot better."[17] Yet today, when these same people want a traditional dish like soup beans cooked right, they put it over a slow-burning wood fire in the iron stoves some have saved all these years. Even though there is a recognition of expedience, there is also a recognition of correctness. The idea of correctness may once have applied to architecture as well as food, but it was swept up in the move toward efficiency, prompting the essential symbol of coal's impact in the Head—the box house.

It became generally acknowledged that milled boards reduced construction time, meaning that Dog Hall's sawmill near Upper Caney had an enormous impact upon the Hollybush community, for it made cut boards readily obtainable not only for laying a floor but for building an entire structure. Whipsawing was time consuming, producing too few boards. Using milled boards made building a house a possibility for those with some money, little time, and little help—a growing segment of the population after about 1930. Those living near both the main creek and Highway 80 needed milled boards first, since it was easier for them to journey to the mines and enter the industrial economy. An outward wavelike distribution took place afterward; in the Head it required another fifteen to twenty years for box to become widely accepted, and regarded as convenient and necessary. Once residents began working on the outside, however, the speed that box construction offered became paramount. Austin Slone ex-

plained: "It would have taken longer to hew the logs, you know. Even after you had the logs hewed, you could put the wall up on that box house quicker than what you could notch them logs. Of course, it wasn't all that big of a problem for three to put them logs up there, but you know it took time to go get them. Even after you got them up there, you know, notching them logs in was a pretty good job, getting them notched right."[18]

There was still some persistence in using shaped logs into the 1930s. These houses, however, epitomize overlapping transition, since they were the last hewn ones built before the inclusion of the box house in the Head builders' repertoire. The most telling explanation offered for this inclusion was that in "the old days people had more time than money," but later "they had more money than time."[19] When Austin Slone built his box house (No. 39), he, like many others, was employed in the mines and had money, but neither of the old quotas of time and help. When dwindling available manpower caused workings to be dropped as a social practice, the lighter building material became essential. As another informant put it, box "is cheap and you could do a lot of the work yourself, and in building a log house you had to have house-raising and things like that, you know, and people come in to help you."[20] Milled lumber could be transported easily and erected with the help of only one or two others. Dowl Short moved the materials for his house over Trace with the aid of only a mule and corn sled, as did Austin Slone. Contrast this with the six to eight men needed to cut, snake, hew, and notch logs. The new economic system that drew men out of the Head and away from joint endeavors also supplied the money for them to build with materials that required little cooperative effort.

In terms of actual construction, however, box did share one trait with log that hastened its adoption: the interchangeability of construction units. People in the Head did not see the log building as necessarily remaining in a fixed position, but rather as subject to both movement and restructure. Austin Slone moved the logs from his grandfather's house (No. 4) into his double crib (No. 59). Logs from Green Slone's original home (No. 18) were used to build Boss Slone's single-pen (No. 33). What made this movement possible was that logs were subject to a certain fluidity: the basic units of construction—the cut, measured, and notched log—could be separated, moved to another location, and reassembled, as the logs from John B. Slone's crib (No. 46) were moved and restructured on Ellis Gibson's farm. Logs could even be modified, if necessary, by shortening and renotching them or by lengthening them with a splice. By comparison, the elaborate support structure in a balloon-framed or half-timbered house would have been too complicated even to comprehend in terms of interchangeable construction units. Bricks and stones were comprehensible in these terms, but their sheer numbers would have made the idea undesirable.

The construction of the box house, however, followed the same repetitive system as the log house, only now there were two units: the board and the batten. The number of construction units had doubled but were still readily comprehensible. Dowl Short could easily disassemble a neighbor's house on Trace, move the units to a new site, and reassemble them to duplicate the original form. Marl Huff was able to disassemble his smokehouse (No. 55) and take it with him when he left Hollybush, reassembling it at his new home. Few if any builders in the Head would have attempted this feat with a balloon-frame building because of the difficulty in conceptualizing it in units that could be easily transported and rebuilt. This recognition of interchangeable units is what made box preferable to frame when the transition from log to a new and lighter material was occurring.

Balloon framing was popularized in the area by coal company architects, who built rows of frame dwellings to shelter the growing influx of miners moving into coal camps. Once sawmills and the alternative house model came in, the frame house was a possibility for all,[21] but the ingrained tradition of movable log units and repetitive acts in construction made boards and battens easier to fit into the old conceptual framework. The box-house builders, while saving large quantities of time, could still apply some of the principles once used with log.

Aesthetics also came into place in the adaptation of box. The new material was more readily accepted when it became thought of as attractive. Dowl Short, in discussing his use of milled boards, emphasized that his wife Dovie considered a box house stylish and "had to have one."[22] He readily agreed, since he knew it would be easier than building in log. Austin Slone's wife Florida also thought a box house "looked better," and that by the mid-1930s, "people wanted something different."[23] People in the Head wanted what they saw on the main creeks, particularly since the log house was beginning to be viewed by outsiders as old-fashioned and representative of outdated values. Austin had the idea of building a box house because "I'd seen other [similar] houses [on the outside]."[24] Merdie and Chester Caudill covered the front of their log house (No. 7) to simulate the more fashionable box, as did Jasper Caudill (No. 28). By covering the log room to match the new box one, Chester and Jasper gave their houses visual uniformity, and like everyone else in the Head

who built box facades or houses, they let it be known that their little corner of the world was catching up.

The acceptance of the box house in Hollybush was predicated on the destruction of many of the old ways. It was efficient for men without time; it was easy to construct for men finding themselves without help; it could be paid for with earned wages; and it fulfilled a new sense of aesthetics.[25] Finally, the box house could be heated solely by the mineral that was responsible for revolutionizing and overturning the past.

Coal was first substituted for wood as chimneys moved to the center of the log house. Wood burned cleaner but required much more work to gather. Austin Slone commented, "I'll tell you what, when you burn wood, you've got a full-time job getting wood, especially with an ax and crosscut saw . . . it takes an awful lot of wood. Your coal, well, a half-bushel of coal would burn longer than—well, I don't know—it would outlast four or five sled loads of wood."[26] And while wood required continual gathering, coal needed to be collected only once a year, customarily during the fall; enough coal to meet a family's annual heating and cooking needs, about two hundred bushels, could be mined in about a week. In addition, as more and more land was cleared of trees, firewood had to be hauled to the house from farther and farther away. Lee Hall recalled that by about 1910, "wood was getting scarce. My dad—the wood we used, on what we called new ground—we would haul the wood out of them places where he would clear the ground. You would have to burn a lot of them, you know."[27] The volume of coal needed was smaller than that of wood, and it could be gathered faster, but most important, it was necessary, since the box house was less heat efficient than the log house.

In box houses, the inch-thick planks had only about one-fifth the insulating capability of a hewn-log wall.[28] Cardboard and paper insulation on the inside walls of a box house could cut the BTU loss from five times that of a log house to about three, but even so, the prospect of heating so thermally unfit a house with wood seemed an impossibility. If heating a log house with wood was considered a full-time job even when the forests were closer, then the amount of wood, time, and labor necessary to maintain a livable temperature in a box house during winter months would have been at cross-purposes with the time- and labor-efficient goals of the construction method. Coal made heating the box house possible. A pound of bituminous coal of low to medium volatility has a BTU value of about 15,000. A pound of wood, depending on the variety and moisture content, averages about 4,500 BTU.[29] Coal provides, then, on a comparative weight basis, a little over three times the heat of wood. In a box house insulated with cardboard and paper, the heat loss, three times higher than log, could be compensated for by burning coal, three times more efficient than wood.

Why not burn coal in a heat-efficient log house and reap both benefits? Many people did, but the decline in available time and help for building and the changing attitude toward log houses made the box house inevitable. The box house thrived on changing values and was representative of their glory. Even its inefficiencies could be compensated for in the new order. If it could not keep the cold out, more of the seemingly endless supply of coal could be heaped on its fires.

The first day a coal merchant came into the area and bought a farmer's coal rights, he brought attention to the black stuff peeking out along the hillsides by attaching a monetary value to it. From that point on, the box house—or one with its capabilities—was assured. It seems doubtful, though, that people in the Head could have predicted that it would feed on their traditions. Each new step toward industrialism and consumerism made the log house more and more a cultural antique, while the box house miraculously seemed to meet all new housing requirements. By the mid-1930s most men must have breathed a sigh of relief when they discovered that a neighbor was going to build a box house. A round-log house, however quickly it could be erected when compared to a hewn one, still required help; the box house did not. Men were free, finally, to pursue outside interests without the associated guilt of abandoning their neighbors' needs. When a man chose to build a box structure, he was aware of his neighbor's sentiments. The box building freed his neighbors from helping and him from needing their help. The individual could now shoulder most of the responsibilities once spread over the entire community. Willard Caudill could built his house (No. 36) with only the help of his brother, who was paid with a calf for his lost time. The communal system had collapsed, and the knowledge of how to build in log no longer needed to be passed on.

It was this ability to have more individual control over the jobs they held, their daily activities, and the structures they built that led to the increased compartmentalization of interior space. Mary Sparkman recalled living (and having company) in a one-room house:

We didn't have any living room. All the beds, just as many beds as you could get in a room, were in that one room. You know, nobody had a separate room. We just grew up together. . . . Back then all your cousins and all would all come in and have the best time ever was. We'd have bean stringings and a lot of people playing. There would be chairs everywhere, you know. And there'd be a memorial out in the cemetery, and so many people would come. Back then they would come about Thursday because, you know, they had to

come in wagons pulled by mules. They couldn't drive their cars there; they had to come way beforehand.[30]

By the mid-1930s people could no longer pay extensive visits because of commitments to outside employment, and most families were no longer living and sleeping in the same room. Austin Slone recalled the logic of his decision in the mid-1940s to section off his home (No. 39) into five rooms: "Well, you know, we needed that much room, the family. You know, their rooms [the older log builders], they built them big, bigger than what these rooms was. I thought I would rather have more rooms, and small." Interviewer: "Just so everybody could get off to themselves?" Austin: "Yes."[31]

This new practice of seeking private moments suggest how far the residents had emotionally moved toward "mainstream" life nearer the main creek; they were making many of the emotional adjustments necessary to cope with an increasingly complex world. I do not know whether the residents knew, by around 1940, that the community was ultimately going to fail; but they seemed, by partitioning space, to be preparing themselves for such a possibility. If individual initiative was needed to survive in the industrial economy, reliance on communal values was seen as meager preparation for the changes quickly moving into view. The ability to subjugate individual will for the well-being of the group was no longer the virtue it had once been. It took a great deal of mettle to leave the safe confines of the Head and look for outside work, to leave the familiarity of home, family, and friends and strike off for the distant Michigan factories as many did. In relation to all the new alternatives that opened up to residents leaving Hollybush, the partitions in their houses surely did not harm them. Apportioned space provided the chance to be alone and to plan a course of action that would take many residents out of the mountains entirely. It took courage to build more rooms of smaller size and to erect partitions when the apparent comfort of a group was juxtaposed against the frequent insecurity of being alone. Compartmentalized space was a subtle message from parents to children that group responsibility was being replaced with individual responsibility, that children needed to pull themselves away from parents and family sooner and more completely than ever before. The partition was the prelude to separation, both actual and emotional.

People in the Head moved from one standard of social behavior to another in a space of only thirty years. When the community finally faded in the late 1950s, residents were better prepared for what awaited them outside Hollybush. They began living near people with whom they were unfamiliar, without the unoccupied space that used to surround them in the Head, in houses grouped tightly along the main roads and creeks. These people now needed to fit into a system as individuals rather than as a collective group. Other people in the area had a twenty- to thirty-year head start. While building smaller rooms and partitions was symptomatic of changing relationships and expectations, it was also aimed at closing this temporal gap.

For generations the pattern of living in the Head had been based on subsistence farming. When Tandy Slone moved from one farm site to another, from Caney to Hollybush, he did not necessarily improve his economic situation; he simply took the same skills and outlook from one place to another and repeated traditional processes. By the late 1930s the Head inhabitant could no longer afford to maintain this world view and still expect to fit into the new system. Rather than, like Tandy, looking at a future vested in a new piece of timber land, he needed to anticipate a future of economic gain and perhaps upward mobility, and his architecture began to reflect this neoteric gaze. Although Boss Slone, for example, liked a log house "better than any other kind," he moved finally into a box house (No. 34) as a concession to both outside fashion and the future.

Hawk Slone and young Chester Caudill lived on the same site (Nos. 17 and 41) at separate periods, yet the different ways they constructed their chimneys reflected their dissimilar approaches to life. The site itself is a small spit wedged in between the creek and the hillside. When Hawk lived there in the 1910s, he gardened "a few roasting ears" and had no outbuildings. Hawk lived on the principle of not looking too far into the future or of building structures based on yearnings. His house had one room, and his chimney one opening. Only when Hawk's situation changed did he plan an alternative course of action. By the time Chester built his house in the late 1940s, hewn logs had given way to boards and battens. The principal difference between Hawk's and Chester's homes, though, was that Chester thought to leave the back of his chimney open, and Hawk did not. Chester planned for the future and made his intentions known: whenever the need might arise for an additional room, the location had been picked and the heat source prepared. That there would be a new room was not in question, only when it would be built. The exposed firebox gave credence to his dreams and made it obvious to others as well as himself that he intended to prosper. Chester was stating that he was a part of the new system of rising expectations. Dowl Short took the same oath when he left an outside firebox on his box house (No. 34).

When Green Slone, Jasper Caudill, Chester Caudill, and Ellis Slone covered the fronts of their log houses with milled boards, they gave tacit approval to these rapidly transforming values. They wished their houses to look like the newer ones; they incorporated fashion and the future into structures whose very log walls were steeped in the pragmatic values of the past. Box houses may not have been as warm as log, but everyone who wished to express his membership in the new order wanted one, even if it meant only building a frontal facade. When Wiley and Ada Caudill returned from Ohio, they quickly changed their round-log house (No. 42) to approximate as best they could the northern industrial preference. Informants thought Wiley's the most attractive house in the Head, judging it not on the workmanship of the logs or chimney stones, but on its ability to envision the future, or at least come to grips with the ever-changing present. It was a "modern-looking" house that both impressed the lookers and whetted their appetites for life on the outside.

By the late 1940s electricity had come into the Head. Ellis Slone best summed up its influence when he recalled that as soon as it arrived, he immediately had it hooked up to his house (No. 24) and purchased an electric refrigerator. Ellis now had both a utility bill and installment payments to meet each month—new obligations that meant he could no longer afford to stay in the Head.

As early as the mid-1940s people had begun drifting out. Birchel Slone (No. 37) wanted the opportunities and conveniences of the new life. Golden Slone left when he could no longer stand the travel time to and from his job in Wayland. Meredith Slone stated that her husband Vansel wanted to leave "to go out and find a job." Vansel added: "Now that is why we came out. And of course that is why the rest of them came out. There was nothing in there, only what people could farm and make. No work or nothing."[32] Vansel did not begin industrial labor until he was forty-two years old. How that must have shocked his agrarian soul.

Another important motive for people to leave was to make it easier for their children to attend school. The Caney Creek Community Center school had been open since the early 1920's and had had a profound influence on Head residents, particularly since it was only four miles away straight over the mountains and close enough for some of the older children to attend during the week, coming home only on weekends. Education also fit well into the new world view of Head residents. If the communal system, with its steady transference of folk knowledge, was over, what better way to prepare children for contemporary life than through regular formal education? It would give them intellectual skills and prepare them for a future of aggressive upward mobility. Hollybush culture was changing at an almost incomprehensible rate, and learning to shape well-fitting, half-dovetailed logs and to plant "by the signs" no longer seemed so important. Children needed preparation for a new society where the knowledge of things was stressed more than the knowledge of ways.

Verdie Huff (No. 14) recalled, "We moved out to get the children to school. . . . It seems like back in them days children just simply wasn't interested in going to school like they are now. We always had to work and make our food and what we ate. We couldn't buy much at that time. That's what made us leave Hollybush."[33] One of Austin Slone's reasons for leaving was so that his children could continue to attend school; the same was true for his brother Boss. Ellis Slone was so enamored of education as a necessary preparation for the future that he enrolled in vocational school when he was in his forties. By 1953 it no longer seemed sensible to him, however, that he and his children should walk out of the Head to work and high school each day. Ellis recalled:

I moved on account of the school. Now you know it's come, more people needed to be educated, and I wanted—I didn't get no education much—I had to walk a long ways, I was raised in the head of this hollow right here [Sparkman Branch], and I had to walk down here to school, and I was trying to get my kids educated. That's what I had in mind; regardless of what it cost, I wanted it done. I figured I had to work, and there wasn't no use in them walking out, and I thought I'd move out and get closer to the school.[34]

A one-room school was built in the Head in 1942 (No. 68) primarily because parents were troubled that their children needed to walk so far to attend surrounding schools. An agreement with the local school board was reached: if the community would put up the building, the school board would supply windows and roofing material and provide a teacher. Box construction had long since made its way into the Head, but it was not used to construct the school, even though schoolhouses on the outside were being built with boards and battens long before 1942. Instead, Head residents cut huge oaks, chestnuts, and pines from high up on the ridges, snaked them down to the site, shaped them, and erected them—all as a result of a community-wide working. Workings had stopped by then, yet nearly everyone turned out for this particular one. Ellis Slone recalled, "Now when we built that schoolhouse, we hewed them. We built that free of charge, too. We didn't get a dollar out of that. I got the contract. I looked at that the other day, someplace here. I made the man sign it, that he would teach in it. Before I said the people would work [build] it, you just sign the contract."[35]

There was nothing unusual about the community's wishing to support the school, but many residents were employed, and the concept of time well spent leaned away from working with hewn logs and group building.

It would have been more practical for each family to contribute a portion of the money necessary to buy milled lumber (which then sold for $25 per 1,000 board feet) and hire a few Head residents to build it. But they did not. The whole community turned out to build this most optimistic of structures—a school—of hewn logs, as if the material somehow needed to fit the occasion. Box was not a suitable material; for this last extensive group effort, the recognition of durability resurfaced. Box could not properly demonstrate time well spent. It could not show, structurally or symbolically, the care and sincerity that parents, on this occasion, wanted to exhibit for their children. Even if time was no longer thought well spent cooperatively building houses, it was—this last time—well spent building a school. Parents wanted their children to continually recognize the effort and care they took in hewing those massive logs. Even the plates were overhung, a technique that had been all but dropped from the builders' repertoire. They did not build in log to save money but rather to impart some symbolic action that was entwined with their history. For this last flowering of the old ways, now quickly being eclipsed, box technology—with its construction methods based on individual action or payment—was rejected for the stability of the past. The school demonstrated through its very existence that parents wanted a structure that represented the future for their children and, vicariously, for them; the hewn logs, however, were intended to remind children of the past, with values of time, care, and cooperation for mutual benefit. The children would be surrounded by these wooden symbols as they immersed themselves daily in the knowledge of outside places, events, and people.

If parents were becoming increasingly aware that the community, because of its location and all the changing circumstances encircling it, was doomed, they were not willing to admit it in this structure. The log school, built to last and based on the old principles of longevity, rocked on the fulcrum between the old and new; its symbolism, housed within its traditionally built walls, seems poignant. The communal system, despite all the cultural conversions in the Head, proved durable—if not in action, at least in memory.

Many informants continue to dream at night that they still live in the Head, dreams that seem to derive from a longing for past security and the feeling of community. Irene Slone stated:

You miss the neighborly part of it. You miss being neighbors; people are not neighbors anymore in the way they were back then in those days when we lived in Hollybush. . . . You get on the phone and you call up a neighbor and see if you can catch him or her home, see if they can be free for an hour or so, and when you went visiting back in those days when I was a child, you didn't—well, for one thing, you didn't have a phone to call, you just went visiting when you took a notion, and when you did go, they welcomed you, you know. It was different from what it is now. . . . I even dream about it sometimes. . . . Oh yes, I still think about Hollybush. I think anybody that ever lived in Hollybush will always remember it as one of the nicest places you could ever live in. To me it is.[36]

Boss Slone added, "If my kids wasn't going to school, I'd be back over there before tomorrow evening . . . I sure would. I'd load my truck up tonight and be over there before daylight in the morning, if it wasn't for my kids going to school."[37]

Not all informants felt this way. Mitchell Slone thought the old life hard, working for 50¢ to $1.00 a day clearing fields and putting up fences. He prefers the conveniences of today.[38] But most former residents view today's conveniences as mixed blessings. Ellis Slone observed, "To tell the truth, I believe we done better then than we do now. The way it is, it's just work from hand to mouth, you know, just work and buy, so many bills. . . . Back then there was nothing to compete with. That $16 house [No. 35] I built was good enough to pass, and now you have to have $50,000 . . . I'll tell you, I believe I lived better then."[39]

Mary Sparkman commented on the changes that occurred not only in the Head but out on the main creek as well:

People from up in Trace where my parents lived, they would get on mules if there was a baby sick with pneumonia, diphtheria, flux, diarrhea, or something like that. That was about all the diseases we knew anything about. They would gather up whole bunches of people and get on mules and go down there and help out. Help the family out if they needed any outside work done, or they would set up with them all night and then come back home. If a person like me . . . got too disabled to work at anything, why, neighbors would come in. They would do my washing, they would clean my house, they'd do anything there was. They'd make my garden. They'd do anything. Now, people don't care for each of them [neighbors]. They are few close families. I mean, I don't know if it's just that they don't have time, and you have to work if you live. If you work, you can't go places like you used to. Well, back then people, when they got their winter coal in, all they had to do was go out there and help somebody.[40]

It is not uncommon to gloss over the past, since it almost always looks cleaner, safer, and more orderly. But Head residents may not be wearing glasses as rose-colored as we might believe. America at large has, in the last half century, only moved from an industrial society of one complexity to another. The same essential values of economic growth, individual determinism, and upward mobility have been maintained, from the mechanized farm to the city or suburbs. Compare that move to the vast changes that occurred in the Head as community cooperation, a barter economy, and concepts of time well spent—which were all used to main-

tain a subsistence agrarian lifestyle—gave way to mainstream values. It is difficult to comprehend the mental adjustments these people have had to make in order to function in the alien system that knocked on their door only fifty years ago. Imagine what the majority of Americans would go through if they attempted to adjust quickly to Hollybush's past agrarian values: the closeness of the extended family, frequent and committed response to the needs of neighbors, and abiding faith that folk tradition would give most of the answers to the questions thought necessary to ask.

By the late 1950s, a steadily declining enrollment caused the county school board to close the school. The stores and gristmills had shut down when Jasper Caudill moved to Michigan and Green Slone died. By early 1960, all the holdouts had drifted from the Head except the families of Austin and Boss Slone. The road out seemed longer and the path over Trace higher than ever before. Soon they too understood that they could not go on. The children needed to go to school, and Austin and Boss wanted to cut their traveling time to work. Austin loaded his family's belongings in a corn sled, locked the front door of his house, and—with his wife Florida and their children—followed the path up to the top of Trace Mountain. They stopped, looked back at their house and farm with sadness, told each other they would come back, turned, and continued down into Trace.[41] Boss was also out within the year. Tandy Slone's great-grandsons had left the area he first settled nearly eighty years before. It was over.

Figure 107. POPLAR TREES BELOW DOWL SHORT'S HOME.

Afterthoughts

The eclipse of architectural custom documented in the Head of Hollybush should serve as an intensified example of the sweeping social impact of coal and industry on communities throughout the region, beginning in the 1890s. What occurred in this mineral-rich area has been understood only in large abstractions: physical displacement and emotional alienation caused the abandonment of the traditional agrarian lifestyle. Hollybush, however, has afforded us a glimpse at the fine print of this process. Over a period of time too elongated for participants to measure, the agrarian rationale was replaced by one aggressively involved with "upward" tangibles; the extended replaced by the nuclear; dependence supplanted by independence. Quite simply, Hollybush no longer perceived itself to be the center of the universe.

If a diffusionary wave is projected out from the commercial mines, this shift of logic, this change in house construction from log to time-expedient boards, should have occurred in less isolated places decades earlier than it did in the Head. According to the Farm House Survey (conducted by the U.S. Department of Agriculture), which examined Knott County dwellings in 1935,[1] it may well have.

The survey indicated that by 1935 almost 75 percent of the county's farmhouses were frame (the surveyors' terminology for any cut-lumber house; informants recall many box houses but few frame at that time). Of that total 66 percent had been built within the preceding twenty-four years, and over half of those (36.1 percent) within the preceding ten years. Since only 26.8 percent of the total surveyed were log, the vast majority built

after 1911 were of boards and battens, which indicates the growing popularity of box structures in the county during a period that coincided with the emergence of the coal industry. This veering toward box strongly suggests that communal systems had broken down all over Knott, if not the surrounding counties, which closely resembled Knott geographically and socially. The impact of industrialism stretched much farther than coal town borders, disrupting the psychic order of isolated societies like the Head's enough to alter values and dominate cultural systems—occurrences which were soon reflected in the designs and techniques used by folk builders. Residents of these communities found themselves in the unenviable position of being anachronous. Their limiting location required shared responsibility, contained aspirations, and a commitment to agriculture. Their newly developing rationale, though, caused them to enviously eye individual gratification and unlimited expectations, to want no more of a commitment to agriculture and each other than a private vegetable garden would require. What life outside had to offer—consumerism, automobiles, houses *not* made of log, current modes of thought—was now more to their liking, easing the inevitable decision to abandon the past.

What future possibiltiies does the combining of oral history and artifactual analysis hold? This has been a regional study which suggests that particular circumstances mirrored specific effects. Using the methodology employed here in another locale might produce different results; rather than charting the impact of industry on a folk society, it might show that a

Figure 108. JOHN L. NOLAN'S FIRST GRAVESTONE.

community in another region has reeled under (or resisted) different social, ethnic, economic, or ideological conditions. What, for example, does the recent history of Cherokee housing in north Georgia tell us about ethnic encroachment? What has been the effect of twentieth-century tourism on the material culture and lifestyle of Anglo-Saxons who washed up on North Carolina's outer banks centuries ago? How have veerings in our cultural perceptions of the moral order, acted out politically and artistically on a national scale, been treated by regional traditionalists? Each situation will exhibit a response to a myriad of contingencies. Folk culture in America has undergone tremendous transformation in the last one hundred years. A synthesis of oral and artifactual sources will begin to blend these small cultural vignettes and reveal much about the emotional process of our own history.

Two divergent examples overlooked by conven-tional record-keeping persist in Hollybush. First, in the head of the second branch, by Dowl Short's house (No. 34), there are six yellow poplars about 2½ feet in diameter and 125 to 150 feet tall (Fig. 107). As the poplars were being sold off years ago, someone must have reserved these 150-year-old trees to build with if the need ever arose. No one in the ensuing years touched these poplars, once the apple of the hewn-log builder's eye. Housing materials had changed, help was not available, and the skills to hew and notch logs of this size had become either forgotten or ignored knowledge. They still stand, reminders of old intent and the obsolescence created by changing ways.

And second, on top of the knoll where the third branch graveyard lies (No. 67), there are two tombstones, both for the same infant: John Nolan, 1959–1960. The original stone (Fig. 108), made of molded cement and hand-lettered by either a relative or neighbor, has been thrown outside the cemetery fence and replaced, after Hollybush's abandonment, with a factory-cut and -inscribed marble headstone (Fig. 109). Someone close to John was pained by the handmade headstone; it became personally imperative to have a ''proper'' one cut later and to switch the stones. The expression of grief carved into the crudely hand-lettered one was, like the faded society from which it evolved, no longer suitable. It was cast aside and replaced by machine precision. Considering all that happened, even this action was inevitable.

Figure 109. JOHN L. NOLAN'S SECOND GRAVESTONE.

Notes

INTRODUCTION

1. P.E. Karan and Cotton Mather, eds., *Atlas of Kentucky* (Lexington: Univ. Press of Kentucky, 1977), 117–19.

2. "A Knott County Issue Celebrating Kentucky's Bicentennial," *Appalachian Heritage* 2–3 (Fall–Winter 1974–75). For an overview of the region, see Thomas R. Ford, ed., *The Southern Appalachian Region: A Survey* (Lexington: Univ. Press of Kentucky, 1962). Eastern Kentucky and its history are fondly described in Henry P. Scalf, *Kentucky's Last Frontier* (Pikeville, Ky.: Pikeville College Press, 1972); C. Mitchel Hall, *Jenny Wiley Country*, 2 vols. (Kingsport, Tenn.: Kingsport Press, 1972); Bernice Calmes Caudill, *Pioneers of Eastern Kentucky* (Cincinnati: Creative Printing, 1969).

3. Descriptions of living communities in Appalachia are extensive: see, e.g., John B. Stephenson, *Shiloh: A Mountain Community* (Lexington: Univ. Press of Kentucky, 1968); George L. Hicks, *Appalachian Valley, Case Studies in Cultural Anthropology Series* (New York: Holt, Rinehart and Winston, 1976); Marion Pearsall, *Little Smoke Ridge: The Natural History of a Southern Appalachian Neighborhood* (University: Univ. of Alabama Press, 1959); James S. Brown, *The Family Group in a Kentucky Mountain Farming Community*, Bulletin 588, June 1952, and *The Farm Family in a Kentucky Mountain Neighborhood*, Bulletin 587, May 1952 (Kentucky Agricultural Experiment Station, Univ. of Kentucky); Marie Campbell, "The Folklife of a Kentucky Mountain Community" (thesis, Southern Illinois Normal Univ., 1937); Harold Warren, " . . . *a right good people*" (Boone, N.C.: Appalachian Consortium Press, 1974), 44–56.

4. For recent explanations of change in Appalachia, see H. Dudley Plunkett and Mary Jean Bowman, *Elites and Change in the Kentucky Mountains* (Lexington: Univ. Press of Kentucky, 1973); John D. Photiadis and Harry K. Schwarzweller, eds., *Change in Rural Appalachia* (Philadelphia: Univ. of Pennsylvania Press, 1970). For broader theories of cultural change, generally combining the effects of westernization and modernization, see Daniel Lerner, *The Passing of Traditional Society* (New York: Free Press, 1958); James S. Stotkin, *From Field to Factory* (New York: Free Press, 1960); Raymond W. Mack, *Transforming America: Patterns of Social Change* (New York: Random House, 1967), especially chs. 1, 2.

5. Henry Glassie, *Folk Housing in Middle Virginia: A Structural Analysis of Historic Artifacts* (Knoxville: Univ. of Tennessee Press, 1975), 10.

6. Folk architecture, or those artifacts built according to local custom out of available materials to shelter people as they go about their daily lives, is expertly explained in ch. 2 of Howard Wight Marshall's *Folk Architecture in Little Dixie: A Regional Culture in Missouri* (Columbia: Univ. of Missouri Press, 1981).

7. Details of conducting an architectural survey can be found in Warren E. Roberts, "Fieldwork: Recording Material Culture," in *Folklore and Folklife: An Introduction,* ed. Richard M. Dorson (Chicago: Univ. of Chicago Press, 1972), 431–44.

8. For some evidence of the artifact's importance in comprehending American history, see Glassie, *Folk Housing in Middle Virginia*; James Deetz, *In Small Things Forgotten: The Archeology of Early American Life* (Garden City, N.Y.: Anchor Books, 1977); John A. Kouwenhoven, *The Arts in Modern American Civilization* (New York: W. W. Norton, 1967); Robert Venturi, Denise Scott Brown, and Steven Izenour, *Learning from Las Vegas: The Forgotten Symbolism of Architectural Form* (Cambridge: MIT Press, 1977); Bernard Fontana, J. Cameron Greenleaf, et al, "Johnny Ward's Ranch: A Study in Historic Archeology," *Kiva* 28:1–2 (Oct.–Dec. 1962), 1–115. Cultural geographers are often able to determine movements in culture and ideas by calculating the diffusion of architectural forms. See, e.g., Fred Kniffen's pioneering effort, "Folk Housing: Key to Diffusion," *Annals of the Association of American Geographers* 55 (1965): 549–77.

CHAPTER 1

1. Irene Slone, interview, May 1979.
2. Oliver Caudill, interview, Oct. 1979.
3. Mitchell Slone, interview, Nov. 1979.
4. Irene Slone, interview, Nov. 1979.
5. Ibid.
6. Kelly Franklin to John C. Slone, 7 March 1890, Book 2, page 77, Knott County Courthouse.
7. Ellen Hall, interview, Nov. 1979. Later deed references and the 7th (1850) Floyd County Census Schedule (dwelling no. 281) support these contentions.
8. John C. Slone to Isaac Caudill, 30 Dec. 1893, Book 6, page 437, Knott County Courthouse.
9. Kelly Franklin to John C. Slone, 7 March 1890, Book 2, page 77, Knott County Courthouse; John C. Slone to Isom L. Slone, 17 Dec. 1897, Book 8, page 66, Knott County Courthouse.
10. John C. Slone to Isom L. Slone, 17 Dec. 1897, Book 8, page 66, Knott County Courthouse; Isom L. Slone to Northern Coal Company, 24 June 1903, Book 13, page 286, Knott County Courthouse.
11. Five studies combining oral history and architecture are George Ewart Evans, *Ask the Fellows Who Cut the Hay* (London: Faber and Faber, 1956); Ormond Loomis, "Tradition and the Individual Farmer" (Ph.D. diss., Indiana University, 1980); George W. McDaniel, *Hearth and Home: Preserving a People's Culture* (Philadelphia: Temple Univ. Press, 1982); Robert R. Madden and T. Russell Jones, *Mountain Home—The Walker Family Homestead* (Washington, D.C.: U.S. Department of the Interior, 1977); Lynwood Montell and Michael Morse, *Kentucky Folk Architecture* (Lexington: Univ. Press of Kentucky, 1976).
12. David M. Pendergast and Clement W. Meighan noted, along these same lines, that contemporary Paiute oral tradition and descriptions about life among their ancestors eight hundred years ago was consistent with archeological evidence then being uncovered, particularly in relation to material culture. See "Folk Traditions as Historical Fact: A Paiute Example," *Journal of American Folklore* 72 (April–June 1959): 130.
13. Interviews with Ollie Craft, May 1979; Verdie Huff, May 1979; Marl Huff, Nov. 1979.
14. In folk architecture nomenclature, a saddlebag house consists of two rooms, no more than one-and-a-half stories high, and built side to side against a central chimney (see Fig. 25, e.g.). A house consisting of only one room is called a single-pen (Fig. 26); a two-room house with a covered walkway between the rooms, and chimneys on the gable ends, is known as a dogtrot (Fig. 27); if no walkway is present and the rooms buttress each other, the house is referred to as a double-pen (Fig. 32).
15. Mitchell Slone, interview, April, Nov. 1979.
16. Ada Caudill and Lou Hattie Hall, interview, July 1979.
17. Vansel Slone, Meredith Slone, Bethel Slone, Marcus Slone.
18. Interviews with Oliver Caudill, Oct. 1979; Irene Slone, Nov. 1979; Mary Sparkman, Nov. 1979. Although this particular occurrence is a family legend, it should not be regarded with less esteem than oral history in terms of veracity. Both are based on perceptions of truth, and a large difference between the two lies in their transmission. Oral history usually entails one person's experiential understanding of events, and does not necessarily pass into verbal tradition. When an event, or perceptions about it, borders on the extraordinary, it may and often does begin to pass from one person to another into oral tradition, becoming a legend.
19. Irene Slone, interview, Nov. 1979.
20. Interviews with Elbert Slone, March 1979; James Huff, April 1979; Ellis Slone, March 1979; Boss Slone, July 1979.
21. Nos. 22, 32, and 37.
22. Isom L. Slone to Northern Coal Company, 24 June 1903, Book 13, page 286, Knott County Courthouse.
23. Interviews with Dowl Short, Aug. 1979; Amanda Hall Adams, March 1979.
24. Interview, 13 Nov. 1979.
25. John C. Slone to U.S. Post Office Department, Washington, D.C., dated 4 Oct. 1902. Lee Hall (interview, Dec. 1979) substantiated Ellen Hall's description of the site, the house, and its partial purpose.
26. Isom B. Slone to U.S. Post Office Department, Washington, D.C., dated 26 Sept. 1906.
27. Mitchell Slone, interview, April 1979.
28. Victoria Watson, interview, April 1979.
29. Harvey Caudill to John B. Slone, 10 Oct. 1910, Book 26, page 294, Knott County Courthouse.
30. Cody Jacobs, interview, Dec. 1979.
31. John D. Slone to Miles Jacobs, 24 May 1926, Book 46, page 460, Knott County Courthouse, Hindman, Kentucky.
32. Boss Slone, interview, July 1979.
33. Mitchell Slone, interview, Nov. 1979.
34. Interviews with Ollie Craft, June 1979; Delia Caudill Taylor, June 1979; Marl Huff, Nov. 1979.
35. Interview, Dec. 1979.
36. Mary Sparkman, interview, Nov. 1979.
37. Hardin and Mahala Slone, Isom and Sarah Caudill to Northern Coal Company, 22 April 1903, Book 13, page 130, Knott County Courthouse.
38. John C. Slone to Isaac Caudill, 20 Aug. 1893, Book 6, page 437, Knott County Courthouse.
39. Isaac and Judy Caudill, Isom and Sarah Caudill to Franklin Caudill, 5 Aug. 1905, Book 10, page 574, Knott County Courthouse.
40. However, two old deed references were unsubstantiated through oral testimony. One deed mentions a Phelix Thomas house as possibly having been in the Head as early as 1886 (Isaac and Judy Caudill to J. D. Slone, 30 Aug. 1893, Book 8, page 523, Knott County Courthouse). No one interviewed had ever heard of a Thomas living anywhere in the Head, county deedbooks show no ownership by Phelix in Hollybush, nor do grant and patent deeds. The Thomas family, however, has owned land on the Mallet side of the mountain for over one hundred years.

The other orally substantiated deed reference (Wyatt Martin to J. C. Slone, 21 Feb. 1889, Book 3, page 480, Knott County Courthouse) concerns the Robert Amburgey "deadening"; that is, a clearing formed by killing live trees by stripping the bark off a lower section all the way around them. An R. H. Amburgey lived three miles to the north (Columbia Gas Company line map, approximately 1904, Prestonsburg, Kentucky) and probably cleared the land to farm, not necessarily to build on.

It was not uncommon to farm land on which one did not live. The following agreement (dated 24 Feb. 1860 and spelled as shown) outlines such an arrangement in middle Hollybush in 1860:

> An artickle of agreement made between Isom Slone of the one part wee Wm Vanover Jr. and Wm Vanover sr of the other part the said Isom Slone doth bind himself to let tham have his holly Bush land three years to tend and wee doth bind ourselves to threw down and put one new rail next to the Bottom ones. They also Bind themselves to put his farm under a good nine rail fence out of white oak yalow popular and chestnut timber and put no rotton rails in his fence and they Bind themselves not to sell their contract to noone else. . . .

41. Interviews with Ollie Craft, May 1979; Delia Caudill Taylor, May 1979.

42. Marl Huff, interview, Dec. 1979.

43. Nov. 1979.

44. Interview, Nov. 1979.

45. Mary Sparkman recalled that Tandy was said to have arrived in January, not in July, as the deed states. The journey to faraway Prestonsburg Courthouse to register the transaction must have required warmer weather and drier roads, causing the transfer to be postponed.

46. William and Polly Triplett to Tandy Slone, 22 July 1881, Book K, page 470, Floyd County Courthouse.

47. William Lynwood Montell, *The Saga of Coe Ridge* (Knoxville: Univ. of Tennessee Press, 1972), 192–97.

48. Irene Slone, interview, April 1979.

49. Lou Hattie Hall, interview, June 1979.

50. Boss and Zona Slone, interview, July 1979.

51. Interview, Nov. 1979.

CHAPTER 2

1. Much of the information on house construction came from three informants: Austin and Boss Slone, great-grandsons of Tandy Slone; and Cody Jacobs, who as a young man watched log houses being built and has remained a practicing student of the "old timers" and their ways for over half a century.

2. Interview, Feb. 1980.

3. Hobart Watson, interview, Dec. 1979.

4. Cody Jacobs, interview, Dec. 1979.

5. Boss Slone, interview, July 1979.

6. The early hewn-log houses in Knott County had full-dovetail notching, demonstrating Pennsylvania German influence in southeastern Kentucky. Often, an extra inward and downward angle was cut into the dovetails. The logs could then be taken apart only by lifting each one straight up. One informant (Sterling Martin, interview, Nov. 1979) witnessed coal company bulldozers trying to push such a house down. The full-dovetailed corners held so tightly that the house was torn off its foundation and skidded across the ground without its logs' loosening. The bulldozing was finally abandoned, and the logs were pulled up one by one.

7. Since the trees from which the puncheons were cut tapered from bottom to top, the split trunks were cut to the smaller measurements. If a board, for example, was 16 inches wide and 4 inches thick on one end, and 12 inches wide and 3 inches thick on the other, the builder would then cut into the grain so that the finished puncheon was 12 inches wide and 3 inches thick.

8. Ellen Hall, interview, 11 Nov. 1979. Cutting boards with a whipsaw (or pit saw) is a building practice dating back to Roman times; see Henry O. Mercer, *Ancient Carpenters' Tools* (Doylestown, Pa.: Bucks County Historical Society, 1960), 16–17.

9. Cody Jacobs, interview, Dec. 1979.

10. Austin Slone, interview, Feb. 1980.

11. An excellent illustrated description of this process, and of the hewing technique, appears in *The Foxfire Book 1*, ed. Eliot Wigginton (Garden City, N.Y.: Anchor Books, 1972), 41–52.

12. If the builders of the John C. Slone House (No. 5)—the only house in the Head with a sleeping loft—followed local tradition, the ceiling joists were made of cucumber (*Magnolia acuminata*), chosen because it was a soft enough wood to be shaped and handled overhead more easily than the heavy oak used below. It was not as strong as oak, but the loft floor never had the traffic of the lower one. Unlike the sleepers, ceiling joists were square-notched into the logs when the log wall reached a height of about 7 feet. Once the joists were set in place, the walls were continued up for another 4 to 5 feet, creating the half wall for the upper story. Poplar and buckeye, other softwoods easily worked with bladed tools, were used for floorboards. Buckeye was never used for the lower floor because it could not be cleaned with sand as could poplar, and it wore out more quickly.

13. The central piercing followed Henry Glassie's structural grammar for middle Virginia houses (rules 111B to 111B.26.2); see Glassie, *Folk Housing in Middle Virginia*, 27–28.

14. Henry Glassie has documented the use of framing boards throughout much of the upland South; see "Southern Mountain Houses: A Study in American Folk Culture," (thesis, State Univ. of New York at Oneonta, 1965), 72.

15. This supports Warren Roberts's contention that windows were often fashioned by the folk builder at Indiana house sites; see "The Tools Used in Building Log Houses in Indiana," *Pioneer America* 9 (July 1977), 32–61.

16. See Nos. 8, 33, e.g.

17. See Nos. 9, 10, 12, 18, 24, 30, 42.

18. See No. 18.

19. Boss Slone's house (No. 43) has its plate set perpendicular; the plate in Wiley Caudill's round-log room (No. 19) is parallel.

20. Box construction has previously been described in Walter R. Nelson, "Some Examples of Plank House Construction and Their Origin," *Pioneer America* 1 (July 1969): 18–29; Dianne O. Tebbetts, "Traditional Houses of Independence County, Arkansas," *Pioneer America* 10 (June 1978): 37–55.

21. The practice of framing the box house in the corners and on the sides of doors and windows may derive from English half-timbered construction. Tex Ballance, a building contractor from Hatteras, North Carolina, first settled by the English in the seventeenth century, recalled as a boy helping older men disassemble half-timbered houses framed in exactly the same manner as this Appalachian box (interview, June 1981). An eighteenth-century English Small House utilizing a similar framing technique is shown in R. W. Brunskill, *Illustrated Handbook of Vernacular Architecture* (New York: Universe Books, 1970), 69(d).

22. Boss Slone, interview, July 1979.

23. Austin Slone (No. 39), Boss Slone (No. 43), Ellis Slone

(No. 24), and Elbert Slone (No. 34) all commented on the aesthetic value of roof tins.

24. Meredith Slone (interview, Oct. 1979) recalled that her mother had spoken of papering walls in about 1900. The practice may extend back much further: the oldest wallpaper located in the area, in terms of publication date, was from an 1833 edition of James Fenimore Cooper's, *The Pioneers* (it could have been applied much later, of course). Papering, once popular throughout the rural American South, Midwest, and West, may have antecedents in the British Isles. In Scotland, whitewashed newspaper was used to smooth over a rough wooden wall. Occasionally, the newspaper was left unpainted, covering the wall or the headboard of an enclosed box bed in even rows (letter from R. W. Smith, Curator, Auchindrain Museum of Country Life, Argyll, Scotland to Charles E. Martin, 6 January 1982).

25. Rilda Watson, interview, Oct. 1979.

26. Florida Slone, interview, Nov. 1979.

27. Alberta Madden, interview, Oct. 1979.

28. Lou Hattie Hall, interview, Oct. 1979.

29. Verna Mae Slone, interview, Oct. 1979.

30. Interview, Oct. 1979.

31. Alberta Madden, interview, Oct. 1979.

32. Irene Slone, interview, Oct. 1979.

33. Irene Slone, interview, Dec. 1979.

34. Interview, Nov. 1979.

35. Betty Huff, interview, Oct. 1979.

36. Mary Sparkman, interview, Nov. 1979.

37. Ben Shahn has documented instances of newspaper lacing used by black Americans in Louisiana to decorate their homes; see FSA-OWl Collection, Library of Congress USF 33–60 18–MZ.

38. Interview, Nov. 1979.

39. Interview, Oct. 1979.

40. Oliver Caudill, interview, Oct. 1979.

41. Some builders purposely placed braces on the outside of barn doors to prevent the stock in the stalls from kicking the doors apart.

42. Henry Glassie writes of the harr-hung door's long history in "Southern Mountain Houses," 120–21; R. W. Brunskill illustrates a medieval example in *Vernacular Architecture*, 123(i).

43. When geography allowed (as often it did not in Hollybush), the farm house and outbuildings were frequently lined up with their ridge lines parallel or at right angles to each other; see, for example, Henry Glassie, "Eighteenth-Century Cultural Process in Delaware Valley Folk Building," in *Winterthur Portfolio* 7 (1972): 51–52, 54; Howard Wight Marshall, *Folk Architecture in Little Dixie*, Figs. 4–2 and 4–4; Thomas Carter, "The Joel Cock House: Meadows of Dan, Patrick County, Virginia," *Southern Folklore Quarterly* 39 (1975): 332, Fig. 3.

CHAPTER 3

1. Eastern Kentucky is part of a folk architectural area that extends along the Cumberland Plateau and includes much of West Virginia, western Virginia, and eastern Tennessee. The architectural sample of single-pens, double-pens, saddlebags,

and barn types that the Head of Hollybush gives is part, then, of a much wider complex, southern in orientation, which has analogues elsewhere. Although many of eastern Kentucky's folk traditions, especially in music and crafts, have been seriously treated by scholars, folk housing has been largely ignored. Henry Glassie has given comprehensive treatment to the expanses east of the Cumberlands, and much of his data on log house and barn types, dimensions, and building techniques can be applied to the Cumberland Plateau: see "The Types of the Southern Mountain Cabin," in *The Study of American Folklore*, ed. Jan H. Brunvand (New York: Norton, 1968), 338–70; "The Appalachian Log Cabin," *Mountain Life and Work* 39 (1963): 5–14; and "The Old Barns of Appalachia," *Mountain Life and Work* 40 (1965): 21–30. Descriptive studies that specifically deal, even if only in part, with folk architecture along the Cumberland Plateau are Ronald C. Carlisle, *An Architectural Study of Some Log Structures in the Area of the Yatesville Lake Dam, Lawrence County, Kentucky* (Huntington, W.Va.: U.S. Army Corps of Engineers, 1978); Carlisle, *An Architectural Study of Some Log Structures in the Area of the Paintsville Lake Dam, Johnson County, Kentucky* (Huntington, W.Va.: U.S. Army Corps of Engineers, n.d.); Ronald L. Michael and Ronald C. Carlisle, *Historical and Architectural Study of Buildings and Artifacts Associated with the Bulltown·Historic Area, Burnsville Lake Project, Braxton County, West Virginia* (Huntington, W.Va.: U.S. Army Corps of Engineers, 1979); Montell and Morse, *Kentucky Folk Architecture*; Norbert F. Riedl, Donald B. Ball, and Anthony P. Cavender, *A Survey of Traditional Architecture and Related Material Folk Culture Patterns in the Normandy Reservoir, Coffee County, Tennessee* (Knoxville: Univ. of Tennessee Dept. of Anthropology, Report of Investigations no. 17, 1976). These descriptive data (including what appears in this chapter), while not the objective of this study, can be juxtaposed with Glassie's works cited above, with the broader survey he and Fred Kniffen conducted in the 1960s—see "Building in Wood in the Eastern United States: A Time-Place Perspective," *Geographical Review* 56 (Jan. 1966): 40–66—and with other works such as Edna Scofield, "The Evolution and Development of Tennessee Houses," *Journal of the Tennessee Academy of Science* 11 (1936): 229–240; E.J. Wilhelm, Jr., "Folk Settlement Types in the Blue Ridge Mountains," *Keystone Folklore Quarterly* 12 (Fall, 1967): 151–174; Stanley Willis, "Log Houses in Southwest Virginia; Tools Used in Their Construction," *Virginia Cavalcade* 22:36–47; Eugene M. Wilson, "The Single-Pen Log House in the South," *Pioneer America* 2 (1970): 21–28; and Wilbur Zelinsky, "The Log House in Georgia," *Geographical Review* 43 (April 1953): 173–93, all giving a strong indication of the similarities and dissimilarities between Hollybush and other folk architecture throughout the upland South.

2. Mary Sparkman, interview, Nov. 1979.

3. Mary Sparkman, interview, Nov. 1979.

4. Mary Sparkman, interview, Nov. 1979.

5. Austin Slone, interview, May 1979; an agreement between Beaver Creek Coal Company and Adam Slone, book 18, page 359, Knott County Courthouse, dated 1 Nov. 1905, lists the position of Adam's farm.

6. When a family built a house on the site of their previous one, they normally solved logistical problems by living with relatives close by until construction was nearly completed.

7. Ellen Hall, interview, Nov. 1979.

8. Postmaster application by John C. Slone, dated 4 Oct. 1902.

9. Postmaster application by Isom B. Slone, dated 26 Sept. 1906.

10. The early years of this house remain shadowy, since no informants can pinpoint the builder or construction date with any certainty. John B. Slone bought the property in 1910 (Harvie [sic] and Mahala Caudill to John B. Slone, 10 Oct. 1910, Book 26, page 294, Knott County Courthouse), but three of his children say the house was already standing, although to them it did not appear very old (interviews with Merdie Caudill, April 1981; Mitchell Slone, June 1979; Victoria Watson, April 1979). Harvey Caudill owned the property before John B., and Isaac Caudill before Harvey. Either could have constructed the house, but building details point away from Isaac: the logs at No. 7, a house Isaac built, have been worked wider than these; in No. 6 the notches are flush at the corners, but the notches on No. 7 overhang a few inches; No. 6's rooms are rectangular, whereas No. 7 is nearly square.

11. Mitchell Slone, interview, Nov. 1979.

12. Isaac and Judy Caudill, Isom and Sarah Caudill to Franklin Caudill, 5 Aug. 1905, Book 10, page 574, Knott County Courthouse.

13. Delia Caudill Taylor, Hardin's daughter, recalled via family history (interview, June 1979) that the north room of this dogtrot stood before Hardin bought the property from his father, (Isaac and Julia Ann Caudill to Hardin Caudill, 10 April 1902, Book 12, page 163, Knott County Courthouse).

14. A Columbia Gas Company map drawn about 1904 shows his farm to be the largest in the Head.

15. Merdie Caudill, interview, April 1981.

16. Hardin and Mahala Slone to Isaac Caudill and Isom Caudill, 2 March 1903, Book 12, page 123, Knott County Courthouse.

17. John D. and Anna Slone to Isom L. Slone, (n.d.) 1904, Book 35, page 87, Knott County Courthouse.

18. Isom L. Slone to John Huff, 3 Feb. 1925, Book 44, page 124, Knott County Courthouse.

19. Interviews with Mitchell Slone, April 1979; Merdie Caudill, April 1981.

20. Conard Slone, interview, Oct. 1979.

21. Interviews with Ellen Hall, Delia Caudill Taylor, Mitchell Slone, Boss Slone, Austin Slone. See also Commodore Slone, "A Slone's Eye View of Knott," Appalachian Heritage 2–3 (Fall–Winter 1974–75): 26.

22. Marl Huff, interview, Dec. 1979.

23. Austin Slone, interview, May 1979.

24. Mary Sparkman, interview, Nov. 1979.

25. Mitchell Slone, interview, Nov. 1979.

26. For a parallel, see Kenneth W. Clarke, Uncle Bud Long (Lexington, Univ. Press of Kentucky, 1973).

27. Austin Slone, interview, May 1979.

28. Ada Caudill and Lou Hattie Hall, interview, July 1979.

29. Ibid.; Ada Caudill, interview, Dec. 1979.

30. Vansel and Meredith Slone, interview, Aug. 1979.

31. This is a story popular enough among older country folks to warrant its own motif number.

32. Mitchell Slone, interviews, Nov. 1979; April 1981.

33. Interviews with Oliver Caudill, Oct. 1979; Irene Slone, Oct. 1979; Ada Caudill, Dec. 1979.

34. Interview, March 1980.

35. John and Nancy Huff came into possession of the property that year; Book 44, page 124, 3 Feb. 1925, Knott County Courthouse. John had previously lived in the Head; as a young man (about 1910), he resided with his family in the John C. Slone house (No. 5).

36. Interview, April 1979.

37. Cody Jacobs, interview, Dec. 1979.

38. There may have been windows and a rear door, but no informants recall their positions with any certainty.

39. Lou Hattie Hall, interview, Oct. 1979.

40. Oliver Caudill, interview, Oct. 1979.

41. Marl Huff, interview, Dec. 1979.

42. Golden Slone, interview, Nov. 1979.

43. James Huff, interview, Oct. 1979.

44. Interview, July 1979.

45. Dowl Short, interview, Aug. 1979.

46. Dowl originally moved into the Head in the spring of 1934 after marrying Dovie Huff. The newlyweds temporarily resided in the home of her father, John Huff (No. 24), before moving into the Isom L. Slone house (No. 10) for two years. When their own house was completed, Isom L.'s was designated as the barn.

47. Elbert Slone, interview, May 1979.

48. Interview, June 1979.

49. Irene Slone, interview, October 1979.

50. Marcus Slone, interview, June 1979.

51. Ada Caudill, interview, April 1979.

52. Martin Hall, interview, June 1979.

53. Isom and Pearlie Slone to Austin Slone, 24 Sept. 1946, Book 68, page 356, Knott County Courthouse.

54. Interviews with Austin Slone, April, May, July 1979 and Feb. 1980; Florida Slone, Aug., Nov. 1979.

55. Oliver Caudill, interview, Oct. 1979.

56. Interviews with Ada Caudill, July 1979; Lou Hattie Hall, July 1979.

57. The logs were possibly retrieved from the John D. Slone house (No. 11).

58. Boss Slone, interview, July 1979.

59. There were various farming approaches in the Head of Hollybush. Most older settlers farmed the narrow bottoms after they were cleared: they first felled and trimmed the trees, collected and burned the brush, then called for a "log rolling"—a community activity where neighbors (and their mules) would collect at the caller's farm, snake his trimmed logs to a central site, and pile and burn them. Since clearing land was a physically arduous task, only one to two acres were cleared at a time. Selected trees were sold to the timber merchants (for example, Wyatt Martin to Morrely Tate and Co., 21 June 1886, Book 1, page 165, Knott County Courthouse: four black walnut trees at $1.50 apiece), and others were "deadened," or girdled, by cutting bark away from the lower circumference. This was done for two reasons: first, so that a tree too large and troublesome to cut down would not shade the garden with leaves—walnut leaves, for example, were also thought to exude a moisture that would kill corn (Cody Jacobs, interview, May 1981)—and second, so that the tree would die and season, later to be cut down and used to construct fences, tools, furniture, or coffins, depending on wood type. A favored tree could also be cut down immediately, sawed into lengths suitable for storage in a barn runway or unused stall, and allowed to age.

As bottomland was depleted through repeated planting, more land up the hillsides was cleared and farmed, allowing the lower fields to be used for pasture. Through time, these farmers continued to clear higher "new ground"—prized for its fertility—usually as a winter's chore. Log rolling followed in the spring, allowing more and more of the exhausted and eroded hillside fields below to be pastured (interviews with Austin Slone, Feb. 1980; Marcus Slone, May 1981; Mitchell Slone, May 1981). It was often the area practice to sell land after the ridges had been reached and begin a search for new ground.

The increasing population in the Head and surrounding hollows, and the growing scarcity of unsettled land, forced new-ground farming to decrease and cyclical fallowing, or the "laying out" of fields, to increase. Depending on soil richness, hillside patches were planted for one to three years and then allowed to go to weeds and berry briars for about the same amount of time (Albert Stewart, interview, May 1981). For about the first three years after clearing, a hillside patch was worked only with a hoe. After "laying out" for three more years, many of the tree roots had decomposed enough so that a single-foot plow could thereafter be used to turn the soil (Otis Jacobs, interview, May 1981). Whether or not to put dormant "soil banks" (another term used locally for fallowing) into pasture seems to have depended on individual discretion. During the Roosevelt administration in the 1930s, area settlement schools began distributing agricultural bulletins on Upper Caney with instructions for increasing yields and preventing soil depletion and erosion; sometimes they popularized what were said to be already existing methods (Cody Jacobs, interview, May 1981). One new suggestion to prevent erosion, though, was to plant honeysuckle on fallowing slopes. John Huff, who owned all of the second branch from the 1920s into the 1940s, obviously listened. Honeysuckle has spread from the slope below his house to cover about one-quarter of the branch.

In order to avoid extended fallowing, a few farmers practiced "green manuring": Mitchell Slone, e.g., would sow a field in rye or vetch in the fall; in the spring, when the cover crop had grown to a height of about one foot, Mitchell would turn it under and replant the field in corn. Other farmers rotated wheat and oats with corn or sorghum cane, also avoiding extended fallowing. Oats were an early summer crop, used to feed the mules before the corn matured.

Most families in the Head relied on "laying out" as their principal farming method, requiring about sixteen cleared acres—eight seeded and eight fallow—annually, with each family switching pastures and cultivated fields every three years (Marcus Slone, interview, May 1981). This acreage naturally increased as children grew, married, continued to live on the family farm, and shared the work.

Although fallowing was easier than clearing new ground, the latter still remained popular prior to the 1930s because of the fertility factor, and because it was a male's primary winter task. It took a farmer away from the female-dominated household, gave him a means of passing winter's dark time, and provided a sense of hard labor's accomplishment as the hillsides gradually opened.

60. Interviews, Dec. 1979; Verdie Huff, Jan. 1980.

61. It was not standing when Mitchell Slone moved out of Hollybush, but it was when Conard Slone moved to the farm in 1950.

62. Interview, April 1979.

63. A popular style in the Head and county, it is in essence a two-thirds English barn. The missing stall is omitted because of a lack of proper site space or need. See Henry Glassie, "The Variation of Concepts Within Tradition: Barn Building

in Otsego County, New York," in *Man and Cultural Heritage*, ed. H.J. Walker and W.G. Haag (Baton Rouge: Louisiana State Univ. School of Geoscience, 1974), 184.

64. Interview, Dec. 1979.

65. Interview, Feb. 1980.

66. Interview, July 1979.

67. Marcus Slone, interview, Jan. 1980.

68. Irene Slone, interview, Feb. 1980.

69. Marcus Slone, interview, Feb. 1980. For detailed information on the construction and use of the sled, see Blanton Owen, "The Farm Sled of the Southern Appalachian Highlands: Its Construction, Use and Operation," *Pioneer America Society Transactions* 1980: 25–45.

70. Austin Slone, interview, April 1979. Austin himself thought the animal to be nothing more than an opossum.

71. The 1900 Knott County Census Schedule shows that about eight out of ten adults were unable to read and write. This was the Civil War legacy of eastern Kentucky, which was continually denied funds for education because it had chosen to side with the North, while most of the rest of the state supported the South.

72. Irene Slone, interview, April 1979.

73. Ellis Slone, interview, May 1981.

74. Hobart Watson, interview, Dec. 1979.

75. Interview, July 1979.

76. Manufactured in 1925 by the Witte Engine Works, Kansas City, Mo. The hopper was built by the Trau Machinery Co. in Cincinnati at about the same time. Green and one of his brothers (who lived outside the Head) bought identical hoppers and engines. Although Green's was destroyed, the double survives.

77. Austin Slone, interview, Feb. 1980.

78. Irene Slone, interview, Feb. 1980.

79. Build by the Jasper Engine Co. (address unknown).

80. Oliver Caudill, interview, Oct. 1979.

81. Irene Slone, interview, Feb. 1980.

CHAPTER 4

1. When Green's house was disassembled, some of the notched logs were used in his barn (No. 50), which still exists. His grandson, Austin Slone, recalls no sleeping lofts throughout the three-room house.

2. See Nos. 8, 9, 11, 12, 13, 15, 17, 18.

3. Tandy Slone's (No. 2) was 20 by 20 feet; Adam Slone's (No. 4) 18 by 20 feet; John C. Slone's (No. 5) 20 by 24 feet.

4. Nos. 11, 18, 41, and 43 were 16 by 16 feet; Nos. 13, 16, 27, 31, 36, and 38 were 14 by 16 feet; Nos. 29, 37, and 40 were 15 by 15; and Nos. 17, 26, 33, and 35 were 14 by 14 feet. Nos. 19 (15 by 18 feet) and 21 (16 by 18 feet), built in 1920, and No. 30 (18 by 18 feet), built in 1935, were the exceptions.

5. See Nos. 2, 4, 5, 6, 8, 11, 12, 13, 15, 18, 19, 20.

6. Other examples: in 1935 Green Slone moved from his poplar house (No. 18) into his new one (No. 30), built of pine and oak. The Ellis Slone house (No. 35), built soon after, used chestnut and oak. The John Huff house (No. 24), built in 1925, used some poplar, but the majority of the logs were oak and chestnut. The Birchel Slone house (No. 37), built around 1942, used pine and oak; and the Boss Slone house (No. 43), built in 1949, used poplar (which had begun growing again)

but liberally interspersed it with pine. An early exception to this general pattern is the Isaac Caudill house (No. 7), which is all pine and was built c. 1900: the careful hewing, 1½-story height, 6-foot-wide wood-burning fireplace, legal documentation, and oral testimony all support the early construction date which the choice of wood belies. Patterns are not all-inclusive.

7. No. 4, e.g.

8. Nos. 6, 7, e.g.

9. A round-log room was eventually built alongside Isom Caudill's hewn one (No. 9). Isom Slone, after buying Ad Slone's hewn saddlebag (No. 4) in the mid-1920s, added a round-log kitchen to the rear of the west room.

10. Benny Caudill lived in his father's hewn house (No. 8) before building the first box house (No. 14) in the Head. Austin Slone also lived in a hewn-log house (No. 33) while building a box house (No. 39). Willard Caudill grew up in two separate hewn houses (Nos. 7 and 20) before building a box house (No. 36). Jasper Caudill built one hewn-log house (No. 20), and upon moving into another (No. 6) immediately tore down one of its hewn rooms and replaced it with a box one (No. 28). His son Chester moved onto a site that had once contained a hewn-log house (No. 17) and built instead a box structure (No. 41).

11. See Nos. 10, 19ii, 22ii, 27, 32, 35.

12. See Nos. 48, 50, 59.

13. See Nos. 28ii, 34, 38, 39, 41, 42ii, 42iv, 71, 72, 73, 74.

14. Oliver Caudill, interview, Oct. 1979.

15. Irene Slone, interview, Nov. 1979.

16. Nos. 24, 30.

17. Nos. 24, 30, 34.

18. Figures supplied by Garner Lumber Company, Garner, Kentucky, which sold many of the tins used in the area at that time.

19. The Jasper Caudill farm (No. 20); book 73, page 175, 15 October 1945, Knott County Courthouse.

20. See Nos. 20, 24, 27, 28, 29, 30, 34, 38, 39, 40, 41, 42, 43.

21. See Nos. 19ii, 24, 30, 33, e.g.

22. A collar brace was used in only one structure, a double-stall barn with an overhanging gable, built by Grover Caudill in the 1940s.

23. Nos. 19ii, 24, 30, 34, 42, 43, e.g.

24. Nos. 34, 43.

25. Ellen Hall, interview, Nov. 1979.

26. Interview, Oct. 1979.

27. Interview, Dec. 1979.

28. Some additional examples: Dunk Caudill went, in a relatively short period of time, from no windows (No. 13) to one window for two rooms (No. 27) to three windows for four rooms (No. 38). When Ellis Gibson moved into John C. Slone's house (No. 12) in the 1930s, he thought it necessary to include two windows in the three-walled addition he built, and to cut a window in a wall John C. had been willing to leave blank twenty years earlier.

29. Vansel and Meredith Slone, interview, Aug. 1979.

30. Older informants like Ellen Hall, age 86, and Lee Hall, age 92, recalled few central chimneys in the area prior to about 1910. Archive photos and fieldwork support their contentions.

31. Hardin Caudill, by 1905, added a room onto an existing single-pen (No. 8) to make a dogtrot with end chimneys. When the John B. Slone house (No. 6) was constructed

sometime before 1910, it too had end chimneys, built initially or at different times. John D. Slone moved into a double-pen with end chimneys (No. 11) in the third branch by around 1910.

32. Although coal was first discovered in the 1850s, it was not until the early years of the twentieth century that land companies bought the mineral rights throughout almost all of eastern Kentucky. Two good readings on mining deeds and the impact of commercial mining on the area's people are Laurel Shackelford and Bill Weinberg, eds., *Our Appalachia* (New York: Hill and Wang, 1977), 133–91; Harry Caudill, *Night Comes to the Cumberlands* (Boston: Atlantic Monthly Press, 1962), 70–112. Studies such as Keith Dix, *Work Relations in the Coal Industry: The Hand-Loading Era, 1880–1930* (Morgantown, W.Va.: Institute for Labor Studies, 1977); Willard Rouse Jillson, *The Coal Industry in Kentucky* (Frankfort: Kentucky Geological Survey, 1924), 1–42; and Albert Pearce, "The Growth and Overdevelopment of the Kentucky Coal Industry, 1912–1929" (thesis, Univ. of Kentucky, 1930), 1–86, outline working conditions and the history of the development of the coal industry in the Cumberland Plateau.

33. Benny Caudill used a saddlebag chimney in his house (No. 14) in 1915, John Huff (No. 24) in 1925, Miles Jacobs (No. 26) in 1926; as did Green Slone (No. 30), Arthur Slone (No. 29), Dunk Caudill (Nos. 27 and 38), Grover Caudill (No. 40), Wiley Caudill (No. 42), and Boss Slone (No. 43), all between 1933 and 1949. Birchel Slone tried a modified version when he built his chimney near the center of the long wall (No. 37). Dowl Short (No. 34) and Chester Caudill (No. 41) built complete versions of the chimneys but incomplete versions of the house.

34. Nos. 8, 11, 12, 13, 18, 19 (east side), 20, 24.

35. Nos. 19 (west side), 27, 29, 30, 31, 32, 34, 36, 37, 38, 39, 40, 41, 42, 43.

36. Nos, 2, 4ii, 5, 6, 7, 8, 9, 11, 12, 14, 15, 18, 20, 22.

37. No. 14 is the exception.

38. Nos. 19, 24, 27, 29, 31, 32, 34, 37, 38, 40, 41, 42, 43.

39. Nos. 23, 30, 33, 35, 36, 39, e.g.

40. Anna Slone cooked in her one-room house (No. 2), as did Sarah Slone (No. 5) and Tenia Slone (No. 4). Separated kitchens were also used: Hardin Caudill built a box room in back of his house (No. 8), connecting it with a covered walkway; Isom Slone built a separate round-log kitchen to the rear of his (no. 4); and Isaac Caudill, after building his house (No. 7), used Tandy Slone's home (No. 2) as his kitchen.

41. Miles Jacobs added a three-walled, hewn-log kitchen to the rear of his saddlebag (No. 26) sometime after 1926. Riven boards were also being used for additions by the mid-1920s (Nos. 15, 21, and 35), but as soon as the cash became available, milled boards replaced both logs and riven slats (Nos. 7ii, 7iii, 8iii, 8iv, 12iii, 14ii, 14iii, 20ii, 24iii, 28ii, 29ii, 30, 31, 32, 40ii, 41). The round-log room on the rear of the first Isom L. Slone house (No. 10) predates this temporal framework, but rarely did Isom do what might have been expected of him.

42. Nos. 9, 19, 20, 22 are the exceptions.

43. Boss Slone, interview, July 1979.

44. Ellis Slone, interview, June 1979.

45. Irene Slone, interview, Nov. 1979.

46. Only two houses were built to face out of the hollow after approximately 1910. One was Golden Slone's (No. 31), built in 1935. Golden explained that he wanted to face the

path leading down the first branch and over the mountain into the third. The lay of the land and the distance to the path meant he could not see it from his house, yet the desire to face it was strong enough for him to position his house in that direction. No explanation was given for the positioning of No. 34, the second house.

47. Nos. 17, 21, 22, 25, 26, 40, 42.

48. The additions added along the fronts of Nos. 9, 12, 18, 19, 24ii, 42 were log. Green Slone's (No. 18) was built before milled lumber became available, so his choice of materials was limited to log. The rest, however, were not. No. 20 seems the exception to this rule.

49. Nos. 7iii, 24iii, 30, 40ii, 42iv.

50. Tandy initially doubled his holdings at no extra cost, however. He bought fifty acres of bottom in 1881; later, when he sold much of this acreage, he included the hillsides he had never owned except through occupation and use (Deed Book 11, page 387, 10 December 1900, Knott County, Kentucky).

51. Dowl Short, interview, Aug. 1979.

52. Vansel and Meredith Slone, interview, June 1979.

53. John and Nancy Huff to Dowl and Dovie Short, 9 December 1944, Book 41, page 597, Knott County Courthouse.

54. Interviews with Ellis Slone, July 1979; Nancy Jane Huff, May, Oct. 1979.

55. It should also be noted that John could afford to hire a builder to help construct this appropriate dwelling.

56. Informants supported these contentions by observing that newly married couples were expected to add to their small houses as the need arose.

57. Nos. 9, 10, 12, 15, 17, 20, 21, 25, 31, 32, 33, 35. Four varied in design: No. 25 had a rear chimney; No. 9, a side room later added on; Nos. 17 and 33, no rear addition.

58. Mary Sparkman, Irene Slone, Ellen Hall, Meredith Slone, and Florida Slone all commented on how well families once got along in relatively little space.

59. Interview, Feb. 1980.

CHAPTER 5

1. Irene Slone, interview, May 1979.

2. Interview, Nov. 1979.

3. Florida Slone, interview, Feb. 1980.

4. Interview, June 1979.

5. Ibid.

6. *The Ascent of Man* (Boston: Little, Brown, 1973). The beginnings of man's movement away from rigid class consciousness and toward individual aspiration to wealth, based on labor-saving and time-efficient technology, has been traced back to twelfth-century Europe; see Jean Gimpel, *The Medieval Machine: The Industrial Revolution of the Middle Ages* (New York: Holt, Rinehart and Winston, 1976). For a description of the immediate collision of what is regarded as the modern industrial revolution, beginning in 1760, with Western society as a whole, see Thomas S. Ashton, *The Industrial Revolution 1760–1830* (Oxford: Oxford Univ. Press, 1948). Many other historians and behavioral scientists have dealt with the fragmenting impact of industrialism on the individual and the smaller traditional society without ever coming to grips with what caused members of a traditional society to break away from the group and to see themselves as

individuals willing to rely on technology to give their increasingly singular existence meaning and form: see Elton Mayo, *The Human Problems of an Industrial Society* (New York: Macmillan, 1933); Siegfried Giedion, *Mechanization Takes Command* (New York, 1948); Hector M. Robertson, *Aspects of the Rise of Economic Individualism* (Cambridge, 1933).

7. Henry Adams, *The Education of Henry Adams* (New York: Modern Library, 1931), 381.

8. Vansel and Meredith Slone, interview, Aug. 1979.

9. Ellis Slone, interview, June 1979.

10. Meredith Slone, interview, Aug. 1979. Mary Sparkman (interview, Nov. 1979) recounted her mother's description of making fabric:

You had sheep and in the wintertime everybody would card this wool, you know, shear these sheep and wash it good and dry it in front of the fire and pick all these burrs out of it and then card it . . . and then roll it up and stack it in the chimney corner where it's nice and warm—you had to work where it was warm. And then you would spin on this old-time wheel—Mother had a spinning wheel. And then you would weave. We had this old big huge loom . . . and they'd weave blankets and all this stuff. They'd weave the material and they would make their clothes out of it for winter. They would make their sheets and their pillowcases and their clothing for summer. They would dye it then with walnut bark. Some would wear it white, you know, make sure it's white and dye the trousers brown.

11. Interview, June 1979.

12. Caney Creek Community Center, founded in 1916.

13. Interview, Feb. 1980.

14. Ibid.

15. In Grover's next house (No. 25), he moved the chimney back to the gable end.

16. Interview, July 1979.

17. Florida Slone, interview, Feb. 1980.

18. Interview, Feb. 1979.

19. Florida Slone, interview, July 1979.

20. Lee Hall, interview, Dec. 1979.

21. A check of archive photographs taken throughout Knott County shows few frame houses before 1915 to 1920. Frame was used to remodel houses in the area earlier than 1915, but not on Upper Caney.

22. Interview, Aug. 1979.

23. Interview, July 1979.

24. Interview, Feb. 1980.

25. Silvia Ann Grider has also noticed the relationship between milled-board structures and rapid industrial growth; see "The Shotgun House in Oil Boomtowns of the Texas Panhandle," *Pioneer America* 7 (July 1975): 47–55. The boomtown house differs in construction from the Appalachian box house, though, in that it incorporates framing members in the walls. Richard Pillsbury has done fieldwork with Cherokee Indians in Georgia who also build box houses similar to those in eastern Kentucky. Perhaps worth pursuing here, rather than antecedents to frameless housing, is the connection between vertical-board housing and the twentieth-century industrialization of isolated traditional societies, regardless of heritage.

26. Interview, Feb. 1980.

27. Interview, Dec. 1979.

28. According to the formula $H = [KA(T_2 - T_1)] \div L$ (where H is heat loss, K is the thermal conductivity factor, A is room area, $T_2 - T_1$ is the difference between internal and external temperature, and L is the thickness of the wood), the heat loss in a 16-by-16 foot room constructed of 6-inch hewn oak logs, when the inside temperature is 75 degrees and the outside

temperature 20 degrees Fahrenheit, would be 2,392 BTU over one hour. The figure for poplar, a much softer wood, would be even less. The average heat loss in a similar-sized room with the same temperature differential but constructed of inch-thick planks cut from oak and white pine (two locally popular sawmilled woods) is 12,650 BTU over one hour. The formula is cited in James A. Richards, Jr., Francis Weston Sears, M. Russell Wehr, and Mark M. Zemansky, *Modern University Physics* (Reading, Mass: Addison-Wesley, 1960), 322. Figures for thermal conductivity on the cited wood types were taken from Robert C. Weast and Samuel M. Selby, *Handbook of Chemistry and Physics* (Cleveland: Chemical Rubber Co., 1967), sec. E-5.

29. Gessner G. Hawley, *The Condensed Chemical Dictionary,* 9th ed. (New York: Van Nostrand Reinhold, 1977), 214.

30. Interview, Nov. 1979.

31. Interview, Feb. 1980.

32. Interview, Aug. 1979.

33. Interview, Nov. 1979.

34. Interview, June 1979.

35. Ibid.

36. Interview, May 1979.

37. Interview, July 1979.

38. Interview, Nov. 1979.

39. Interview, June 1979.

40. Interview, Nov. 1979.

41. Florida Slone, interview, March 1980.

AFTERTHOUGHTS

1. Washington, D.C., 1939.

Bibliography

BOOKS

Adams, Henry. *The Education of Henry Adams.* New York: Modern Library, 1931.

Bronowski, Jacob. *The Ascent of Man.* Boston: Little, Brown, 1973.

Brunskill, R. W. *Illustrated Handbook of Vernacular Architecture.* New York: Universe Books, 1970.

Campbell, Marie. "The Folklife of a Kentucky Mountain Community." Thesis, Southern Illinois Normal Univ., 1937.

Carlisle, Ronald C. *An Architectural Study of Some Log Structures in the Area of the Paintsville Lake Dam, Johnson County, Kentucky.* Huntington, W.Va.: U.S. Army Corps of Engineers, n.d.

————. *An Architectural Study of Some Log Structures in the Area of the Yatesville Lake Dam, Lawrence County, Kentucky.* Huntington, W.Va.: U.S. Army Corps of Engineers, 1978.

Caruso, John A. *The Appalachian Frontier.* New York: Bobbs-Merrill, 1959.

Caudill, Bernice Calmes. *Pioneers of Eastern Kentucky.* Cincinnati: Creative Printing, 1969.

Caudill, Harry. *Night Comes to the Cumberlands.* Boston: Atlantic Monthly Press, 1976.

Collins, William E. *Ways, Means and Customs of our Forefathers.* New York: Vantage, 1976.

Deetz, James. *In Small Things Forgotten: The Archeology of Early American Life.* Garden City, N.Y.: Anchor Books, 1977.

Dix, Keith. *Work Relations in the Coal Industry: The Hand-Loading Era, 1880–1930.* Morgantown, W.Va.: Institute for Labor Studies, 1977.

Duerr, William A. *The Economic Problems of Forestry in the Appalachian Region.* Cambridge: Harvard Univ. Press, 1949.

Evans, George Ewart. *Ask the Fellows Who Cut the Hay.* London: Faber and Faber, 1956.

Fitch, James Marston. *American Building: The Environmental Forces That Shape It.* New York: Schocken, 1975.

Ford Thomas R., ed. *The Southern Appalachian Region: A Survey.* Lexington: Univ. Press of Kentucky, 1962.

Gimpel, Jean. *The Medieval Machine: The Industrial Revolution of the Middle Ages.* New York: Holt, Rinehart and Winston, 1976.

Glassie, Henry. *Folk Housing in Middle Virginia: A Structural Analysis.* Knoxville: Univ. of Tennessee Press, 1975.

————. *Pattern in the Material Folk Culture of the Eastern United States.* Philadelphia: Univ. of Pennsylvania Press, 1968.

————. "Southern Mountain Houses: A Study in American Folk Culture." Thesis, State Univ. of New York at Oneonta, 1965.

————. "The Types of the Southern Mountain Cabin." In *The Study of American Folklore,* ed. Jan Harold Brunvand, 338–70. New York: W. W. Norton, 1968.

————. "The Variation of Concepts within Tradition: Barn Building in Otsego County, New York." In *Man and Cultural Heritage,* H. J. Walker and W. G. Haag, 177–235. Baton Rouge: Louisiana State Univ. School of Geoscience, 1974.

Hawley, Gessner G. *The Condensed Chemical Dictionary.* 9th ed. New York: Van Nostrand Reinhold, 1977.

Hicks, George L. *Appalachian Valley, Case Studies in Cultural Anthropology Series.* New York: Holt, Rinehart and Winston, 1976.

Ireland, Robert M. *The County in Kentucky History.* Lexington: Univ. Press of Kentucky, 1976.

Jillson, Willard Rouse. *The Coal Industry in Kentucky.* Frankfort: Kentucky Geological Survey, 1924.

————. *The Kentucky Land Grants.* Baltimore: Genealogical Publishing, 1971.

Karan, P.E., and Cotton Mather, eds. *Atlas of Kentucky.* Lexington: Univ. Press of Kentucky, 1977.

Kouwenhoven, John A. *The Arts in Modern American Civilization.* New York: W. W. Norton, 1967.

Koyee, William C. *Pioneer Families of Eastern and Southeastern Kentucky.* Baltimore: Genealogical Publishing, 1973.

Lerner, Daniel. *The Passing of Traditional Society.* New York: Free Press, 1958.

Loomis, Ormond. "Tradition and the Individual Farmer." Ph.D. diss. Indiana Univ., 1980.

Mack, Raymond W. *Transforming America: Patterns of Social Change.* New York: Random House, 1967.

Madden, Robert R., and T. Russell Jones. *Mountain Home—The Walker Family Homestead.* Washington, D.C.: U.S. Department of Interior, 1977.

Marshall, Howard Wight. *Folk Architecture in Little Dixie: A Regional Culture in Missouri.* Columbia: Univ. of Missouri Press, 1981.

Mercer, Henry O. *Ancient Carpenters' Tools.* Doylestown, Pa.: Bucks County Historical Society, 1960.

Michael, Ronald L., and Ronald C. Carlisle. *Historical and Architectural Study of Buildings and Artifacts as Associated with the Bulltown Historic Area, Burnsville Lake Project, Braxton County, West Virginia.* Huntington, W.Va.: U.S. Army Corps of Engineers, 1979.

Montell, William Lynwood. *The Saga of Coe Ridge.* Knoxville: Univ. of Tennessee Press, 1972.

Montell, William Lynwood, and Michael Lynn Morse. *Kentucky Folk Architecture.* Lexington: Univ. Press of Kentucky, 1976.

Pearce, Albert. "The Growth and Overdevelopment of the Kentucky Coal Industry, 1912–1929." Thesis, Univ. of Kentucky, 1930.

Photiadis, John D., and Harry K. Schwarzweller, eds. *Change in Rural Appalachia.* Philadelphia: Univ. of Pennsylvania Press, 1970.

Plunkett, H. Dudley, and Mary Jean Bowman. *Elites and Change in the Kentucky Mountains.* Lexington: Univ. Press of Kentucky, 1973.

Richards, James A., Francis Weston Sears, M. Russell Wehr, and Mark M. Zemansky. *Modern University Physics.* Reading, Mass.: Addison-Wesley, 1960.

Riedl, Norbert F., Donald B. Ball, and Anthony P. Cavender. *A Survey of Traditional Architecture and Related Material Folk Culture Patterns in the Normandy Reservoir, Coffee County, Tennessee.* Knoxville: Univ. of Tennessee Dept. of Anthropology, Report of Investigations no. 17, 1976.

Roberts, Warren E. "Folk Architecture"; "Fieldwork: Recording Material Culture." In *Folklore and Folklife: An Introduction,* ed. Richard M. Dorson, 281–94, 431–44. Chicago: Univ. of Chicago Press, 1972.

———. "Some Comments on Log Construction in Scandinavia and the United States." In *Folklore Today: A Festschrift for Richard M. Dorson,* 437–50. Bloomington: Indiana Univ. Press, 1976.

———. "The Whitaker-Waggoner House." In *American Folklife,* ed. Don Yoder, 185–207. Austin: Univ. of Texas Press, 1976.

Scalf, Henry P. *Kentucky's Last Frontier.* Pikeville, Ky.: Pikeville College Press, 1972.

Shackelford, Laurel, and Bill Weinberg, eds. *Our Appalachia.* New York: Hill and Wang, 1977.

Slone, Verna Mae. *What My Heart Wants to Tell.* Washington, D.C.: New Republic Books, 1979.

Stephenson, John B. *Shiloh: A Mountain Community.* Lexington: Univ. Press of Kentucky, 1968.

Stotkin, James S. *From Field to Factory.* New York: Free Press, 1960.

Venturi, Robert, Denise Scott Brown, and Steven Izenour. *Learning from Las Vegas: The Forgotten Symbolism of Architectural Form.* Cambridge: MIT Press, 1977.

Warren, Harold. " . . . *a right good people.*" Boone, N.C.: Appalachian Consortium Press, 1974.

Watlington, Patricia. "The Land." In *Kentucky—Its History and Heritage,* ed. Fred J. Hood, 4–14. St. Louis: Forum Press, 1978.

Weast, Robert C., and Samuel M. Selby. *Handbook of Chemistry and Physics.* Cleveland: Chemical Rubber Co., 1967.

Wharton, Mary E., and Roger W. Barbour. *Trees and Shrubs of Kentucky.* Lexington: Univ. Press of Kentucky, 1978.

Wigginton, Eliot, ed. *The Foxfire Book 1.* Garden City, N.Y.: Anchor Books, 1972.

PERIODICALS

Carter, Thomas. "The Joel Cock House: 1885—Meadows of Dan, Patrick County, Virginia." *Southern Folklore Quarterly* 39 (1975): 329–40.

Dorson, Richard M. "Oral Tradition and Written History: The Case of the United States." *Journal of the Folklore Institute* 1 (Dec. 1964): 220–34.

"Early Times (from the *Autobiography of Old Clabe Jones.)*" *Appalachian Heritage* (Knott County issue) 2–3 (Fall–Winter 1974–75): 14.

Fontana, Bernard, and J. Cameron Greenleaf. "Johnny Ward's Ranch: A Study in Historic Archeology." *Kiva* 28 (Oct.–Dec. 1962): 1–115.

Glassie, Henry. "The Appalachian Log Cabin." *Mountain Life and Work* 39 (Winter 1963): 5–14.

———. "The Double-Crib Barn in South Central Pennsylvania." *Pioneer America* 1 (Jan. 1969): 9–16; (July 1969): 40–45: 2 (Jan. 1970): 47–52; (July 1970): 23–34.

———. "Eighteenth-Century Cultural Process in Delaware Valley Folk Building." *Winterthur Portfolio* 7 (1972): 29–57.

———. "The Old Barns of Appalachia." *Mountain Life and Work* 40 (Summer 1965): 21–30.

Grider, Silvia Ann. "The Shotgun House in Oil Boomtowns of the Texas Panhandle." *Pioneer America* 7 (July 1975): 47–55.

Kniffen, Fred. "Folk Housing: Key to Diffusion." *Annals of the Association of American Geographers* 55 (1965): 549–77.

Kniffen, Fred, and Henry Glassie. "Building in Wood in the Eastern United States: A Time-Place Perspective." *Geographical Review* 56 (Jan. 1966): 40–66.

"Knott County Comes into Being." *Appalachian Heritage* (Knott County issue) 2–3 (Fall–Winter, 1974–75): 4.

Marshall, Howard Wight. "Meat Preservation on the Farm in Missouri's 'Little Dixie.' " *Journal of American Folklore* 92 (Oct.–Dec. 1979): 400–417.

Nelson, Walter R. "Some Examples of Plank House Construction and Their Origin." *Pioneer America* 1 (July 1969): 18–29.

Owen, Blanton. "The Farm Sled of the Southern Appalachian Highlands: Its Construction, Use and Operation." *Pioneer America Society Transactions* 1980: 25–45.

Pendergast, David M., and Clement W. Meighan. "Folk Traditions as Historical Fact: A Paiute Example." *Journal of American Folklore* 72 (April–June 1959): 128–33.

Roberts, Warren E. "The Tools Used in Building Log Houses in Indiana." *Pioneer America* 9 (July 1977): 32–61.

Scofield, Edna. "The Evolution and Development of Tennessee Houses." *Journal of the Tennessee Academy of Science* 11 (1936): 229–401.

Slone, Commodore. "A Slone's Eye View of Knott." *Appalachian Heritage* (Knott County issue) 2–3 (Fall–Winter 1974–75): 24–29.

Smith, Hillard H. to Ann Raleigh Eastham. *Appalachian Heritage* (Knott County issue) 2–3 (Fall–Winter 1974–75): 19.

Tebbetts, Dianne O. "Traditional Houses of Independence County, Arkansas." *Pioneer America* 10 (June 1978): 37–55.

Thomas, James C. "The Log Houses of Kentucky." *Antiques* (April 1974): 791–98.

Wilhelm, E.J., Jr. "Folk Settlement Types in the Blue Ridge Mountains." *Keystone Folklore Quarterly* 12 (Fall 1967): 151–74.

Williams, Cratis. "The Appalachian Experience." *Appalachian Heritage* 7 (Spring 1979): 4–11.

Wilson, Eugene M. "The Single-Pen Log House in the South." *Pioneer America* 2 (1970): 21–28.

Zelinsky, Wilbur. "The Log House in Georgia." *Geographical Review* 43 (April 1953): 173–93.

INTERVIEWS WITH AUTHOR

Adams, Amanda Hall. Hindman, Ky., March 1979.

Ballance, Millard F. Hatteras, N.C., June 1981.

Caudill, Ada. Hollybush, Ky., April, Dec. 1979.

Caudill, Ada, and Lou Hattie Hall. Hollybush, Ky., July 1979.

Caudill, Madge. Hindman, Ky., 1979.

Caudill, Merdie. Hindman, Ky., April 1981.

Caudill, Oliver. Lexington and Head of Hollybush, Ky., Oct. 1979.

Cornett, Orcia. Sassafras, Ky., June 1979.

Craft, Ollie. Mallie, Ky., June 1979.

Hall, Ellen. Hollybush, Ky., Nov., 1979.

Hall, Lee. Hindman, Ky., Dec. 1979.

Hall, Lou Hattie. Hollybush, Ky., Oct. 1979.

Hall, Martin. Sassafras, Ky., April, June 1979.

Huff, Betty. Pippa Passes, Ky., Oct. 1979.

Huff, Curtis. Pippa Passes, Ky., Oct. 1979.

Huff, James. Pippa Passes, Ky., April, Oct., Dec. 1979.

Huff, Lillie. Pippa Passes, Ky., April 1979.

Huff, Marl. Hindman, Ky., Oct., Nov., Dec. 1979; Jan. 1980.

Huff, Menifee. Pippa Passes, Ky., March 1979.

Huff, Nancy Jane. Hindman, Ky., May, Oct. 1979.

Huff, Verdie. Hindman, Ky., Oct., Nov. 1979; Jan. 1980.

Jacobs, Allie. Pippa Passes, Ky., Dec. 1979.

Jacobs, Burnis. Pippa Passes, Ky., May 1979.

Jacobs, Cody. Pippa Passes, Ky., Dec. 1979; Jan., March 1980; May 1981.

Jacobs, Otis. Pippa Passes, Ky., May 1981.

Jones, Arthur. Brinkley, Ky., Aug. 1979.

Madden, Alberta. Hindman, Ky., Oct. 1979.

Madden, Charlotte. Pippa Passes, Ky., July, Aug., Sept. 1979.

Martin, Sterling. Cordia, Ky., Nov. 1979.

Martin, Wyatt. Allen, Ky., July 1979.

Pigman, Annabee. Mallie, Ky., April 1979.

Short, Dowl. Dema, Ky., Aug. 1979.

Slone, Austin. Pippa Passes, Ky., April, May, July 1979; Feb. 1980.

Slone, Bethel. Pippa Passes, Ky., Sept. 1979.

Slone, Boss and Zona. Hindman, Ky., July 1979.

Slone, Conard. Ravenna, Ohio, Oct. 1979.

Slone, Elbert. Pippa Passes, Ky., March, April, Nov. 1979; March 1980.

Slone, Ellis. Pippa Passes, Ky., April, May, June 1979.

Slone, Florida. Pippa Passes, Ky., Aug., Nov. 1979; Feb., March 1980.

Slone, Gene Autry. Pippa Passes, Ky., Nov., Dec. 1979.

Slone, Golden. Wayland, Ky., Nov. 1979.

Slone, Irene. Pippa Passes and Head of Hollybush, Ky., Nov., Dec. 1978; Jan., Feb., March, April, May, June, July, Aug., Sept., Oct., Nov., Dec. 1979; Jan., Feb., March 1980.

Slone, Marcus. Pippa Passes, Ky., June 1979; Jan., Feb., 1980; May 1981.

Slone, Meredith. Pippa Passes, Ky., Aug. Oct., Nov. 1979.

Slone, Merkie, Pippa Passes, Ky., July, Sept., Oct. 1979; March 1980; May 1981.

Slone, Mitchell. Pippa Passes and Head of Hollybush, Ky., March, April, June, July, Sept., Nov. 1979; Jan., March 1980.

Slone, Paul. Pippa Passes, Ky., Feb. 1980.

Slone, Ray. Hindman, Ky., Aug., Sept. 1979.

Slone, Silas. Hollybush, Ky., June 1979.

Slone, Vansel. Pippa Passes, Ky., May 1979.

Slone, Vansel and Meredith. Pippa Passes, Ky., June 1979.

Slone, Verna Mae. Pippa Passes, Ky., June, Oct. 1979.

Sparkman, Eliza. Pippa Passes, Ky., May 1979.

Sparkman, Mary. Pippa Passes, Ky., Nov. 1979.

Stewart, Albert. Pippa Passes, Ky., May 1981.

Taylor, Delia Caudill, Mallie, Ky., June 1979.

Taylor, Nannie. Mallet, Ky., July 1979.

Triplett, Garley, Hollybush, Ky., Nov. 1979.

Watson, Crafus. Pippa Passes, Ky., May, July 1979.

Watson, Frank. Pippa Passes, Ky., June, July, Aug., Sept., Oct., Nov. 1979; Feb. 1980.

Watson, Hassel. Pippa Passes, Ky., June 1979.

Watson, Hobart. Hindman, Ky., Dec. 1979.

Watson, Rilda. Pippa Passes, Ky., Oct. 1979.

Watson, Victoria. Trace, Ky., April 1979.

DEEDS

Caudill, Harvey to Isaac Caudill. Deed in Knott County Courthouse, Hindman, Ky. Book 8, page 468, 8 April 1899.

Caudill, Harvey and Mahala to Hardin and Mary Caudill. Deed in Knott County Courthouse, Hindman, Ky. Book 18, page 420, 1 Nov. 1905.

Caudill, Harvey and Mahala to Isaac Caudill. Deed in Knott County Courthouse, Hindman, Ky. Book 6, page 60, 17 Oct. 1892.

Caudill, Harvey to John B. Slone. Deed in Knott County Courthouse, Hindman, Ky. Book 26, page 294, 10 Oct. 1910.

Caudill, Isaac and Julie Anne to Hardin Caudill. Deed in Knott County Courthouse, Hindman, Ky. Book 12, page 163, 10 April 1902.

Caudill, Isaac and Julie to Harvey Caudill. Deed in Knott County Courthouse, Hindman, Ky. Book 15, page 435, 8 April 1899.

Caudill, Isaac and Judy, Isom and Sarah to Franklin Caudill. Deed in Knott County Courthouse, Hindman, Ky. Book 10, page 574, 5 Aug. 1905.

Caudill, Isaac and Judy to J. D. Slone. Deed in Knott County Courthouse, Hindman, Ky. Book 8, page 523, 30 Aug. 1893.

Franklin, Kelly to John C. Slone. Deed in Knott County Courthouse, Hindman, Ky. Book 2, page 77, 7 March 1890.

Gibson, Henry to Isom L. Slone. Deed in Knott County Courthouse, Hindman, Ky. Book 53, page 499, 23 Feb. 1933.

Huff, John and Nancy to Dowl Short. Deed in Knott County Courthouse, Hindman, Ky. Book 41, page 597, 9 Dec. 1944.

Martin, Tandy to Wyate Martin. Deed in Floyd County Courthouse, Prestonsburg, Ky. Book G, page 584, 24 Aug. 1857.

Martin, Wyatt to Morrely Tate and Co. Timber rights agreement in Knott County Courthouse, Hindman, Ky. Book 1, page 165, 21 June 1886.

Martin, Wyatt to J. C. Slone. Deed in Knott County Courthouse, Hindman, Ky. Book 3, page 480, 21 Feb. 1889.

Martin, Wyatt to Tandy Slone. Deed in Knott County Courthouse, Hindman, Ky. Book 3, page 531, 14 Jan. 1889.

Owens, Vincin to Henry Watson. Deed in Knott County Courthouse, Hindman, Ky. Book 10, page 142, 29 Nov. 1903.

Reynolds, Joseph to Hardin Slone. Deed in Floyd County Courthouse, Prestonsburg, Ky. Book E, page 271, 5 May 1845.

Short, Dowl and Dovie to Elbert Slone. Deed in Knott County Courthouse, Hindman, Ky. Book 65, page 184, 10 May 1945.

Short, Wilson and Nancy, Tandy and Aney [sic] Slone to Hardin Slone. Deed in Knott County Courthouse, Hindman, Ky. Book 2, page 73, 22 March 1889.

Slone, Adam to Beaver Creek Coal Company. Agreement in Knott County Courthouse, Hindman, Ky. Book 18, page 359, 1 Nov. 1905.

Slone, Golden and Laura to Vansel Slone. Deed in Knott County Courthouse, Hindman, Ky. Book 73, page 175, 15 Oct. 1945.

Slone, Greenville and Tandy to Morgan Slone. Deed in Floyd County Courthouse, Prestonsburg, Ky. Book K, page 513, 18 Nov. 1881.

Slone, Hardin and Mahala to Isaac and Isom Caudill. Deed in Knott County Courthouse, Hindman, Ky. Book 12, page 123, 2 March 1903.

Slone, Isom to William Vanover, Sr. and William Vanover, Jr. Original document owned by Ray Slone, Hindman, Ky. 24 Feb. 1860.

Slone, Isom and Pearlie to Austin Slone. Deed in Knott County Courthouse, Hindman, Ky. Book 68, page 356, 24 Sept. 1946.

Slone, Isom L. to John Huff. Deed in Knott County Courthouse, Hindman, Ky. Book 44, page 124, 3 Feb. 1925.

Slone, Isom L. to Northern Coal Company. Deed in Knott County Courthouse, Hindman, Ky. Book 13, page 286, 24 June 1903.

Slone, John C. to Isaac Caudill. Deed in Knott County Courthouse, Hindman, Ky. Book 6, page 437, 30 Aug. 1893.

Slone, John C. to Isom L. Slone. Deed in Knott County Courthouse, Hindman, Ky. Book 8, page 66, 17 Dec. 1897.

Slone, John C. and Sarah to Isaac Caudill. Deed in Knott County Courthouse, Hindman, Ky. Book 15, page 578, 6 July 1903.

Slone, John C. and Sarah, Isom L. and Malinda Slone, to Northern Coal Co. Deed in Knott County Courthouse, Hindman, Ky. Book 13, page 266, 24 June 1903.

Slone, John D. to Miles Jacobs. Deed in Knott County Courthouse, Hindman, Ky. Book 46, page 460, 24 May 1926.

Slone, John D. and Anna to Isom L. Slone. Deed in Knott County Courthouse, Hindman, Ky. Book 35, page 87, 1904.

Slone, John D. and Anna to Isom L. Slone. Deed in Knott County Courthouse, Hindman, Ky. Book 44, page 124, 3 Feb. 1925.

Slone, Tandy and Anna to Hardin Slone. Deed in Knott County Courthouse, Hindman, Ky. Book 11, page 387, 10 Dec. 1900.

Slone, Tandy and Anna, Vincin and Lucinda Owens to Adam Slone. Deed in Knott County Courthouse, Hindman, Ky. Book 15, page 199, 7 March 1903.

Tackett, Greenville to Isaac and Preston Caudill. Deed in Floyd County Courthouse, Prestonsburg, Ky. Book 8, page 279, 5 Feb. 1881.

Thomas, F. P. to Morrely Tate and Co. Timber rights agreement in Knott County Courthouse, Hindman, Ky. Book 1, page 167, 19 June 1886.

Triplett, William and Polly to Tandy Slone. Deed in Floyd County Courthouse, Prestonsburg, Ky. Book K, page 470, 22 July 1881.

Triplett, Wilson and Polly to Alexander Caudle. Deed in Floyd County Courthouse, Prestonsburg, Ky. Book N, page 106, 1 Nov. 1881.

GOVERNMENT DOCUMENTS

Kentucky Geological Survey. Aerial Photo, CYB-IDD, 10 July 1962; aerial Photo, no. 1–59, Series GS-TI, 8 March 1952.

Publication Schedules of the Sixth, Seventh, Eighth, Ninth, and Tenth Censuses of the United States, Floyd County, Kentucky; Publication Schedule of the Twelfth Census of the United States, Knott County, Kentucky. Washington, D.C.: National Archives Microfilms Publications, 1967.

U.S. Department of Agriculture. *The Farm House Survey.* Miscellaneous Publication no. 323. Washington, D.C.: GPO, 1939.

U.S. Post Office Department. Proposed Location of Post Office Application, Isom B. Slone, Hollybush, Kentucky, 26 September 1906; Proposed Location of Post Office Application, John C. Slone, Hollybush, Kentucky, 23 September 1902.

PHOTOGRAPHIC COLLECTIONS AND MAPS

Alice Lloyd College Photographic Archives, Pippa Passes, Ky.

Hindman Settlement School Photographic Collection, Hindman, Ky.

Columbia Gas Company line map of Hollybush, Kentucky. Prestonsburg, Ky. office, c. 1904.

Index